MW01088704

# Disciple of Peace

## Alexander Campbell on Pacifism, Violence and the State

Craig M. Watts

Includes as an Appendix
Alexander Campbell's
"Address on War"

Doulos Christou Press
Indianapolis

DISCIPLE OF PEACE:
ALEXANDER CAMPBELL ON PACIFISM, VIOLENCE AND THE STATE



ISBN: 0-9744796-8-3
ISBN - 13: 978-0-9744796-8-2
LCC No.: 200592819

FIRST EDITION

Doulos Christou Press is an independent, ecumenical press committed to publishing works related to radical Christian discipleship. We are a ministry of Englewood Christian Church ( www.englewoodcc.com ) and fall under the organizational umbrella of the Englewood Community Development Corporation.

Doulos Christou Press
c/o Englewood Christian Church
57 North Rural St.
Indianapolis, IN 46201
www.douloschristou.com

# Table of Contents


Acknowledgments .......... 6

Introduction .......... 7

Chapter 1: Influences in Campbell's Pacifism .......... 15

Chapter 2:
The Chief Characteristics of Campbell's Pacifism .... 29

Chapter 3:
Campbell's Eschatology and his Pacifist Ethics ...... 43

Chapter 4:
Millennial America and the Vision of Peace .......... 57

Chapter 5: Pacifism and Relations with the State .......... 67

Chapter 6: War, Slavery and Civil Disobedience .......... 85

Chapter 7: Anti-War, Pro-Capital Punishment .......... 101

Chapter 8: A Future for a Pacifist Past? .......... 115

Appendix:
Alexander Campbell's "Address on War" .......... 137

Index .......... 161

# Table of Contents

# Acknowledgments

I am indebted in a variety of ways to a number of groups and individuals for their contributions to the completion of this book. The first of these is a group of members from First Christian Church (Disciples of Christ) in Louisville, Kentucky to whom some years ago I presented a short series of lectures on Campbell's pacifism. I appreciate both the patience and the thoughtful responses of the participants.

To those who read most or all of the manuscript, offering their insightful comments and correcting my unfortunate errors, I am deeply appreciative. These include: Rhodes Thompson, Lester McAllister, Joe Jones, Philip Kenneson and Lee Camp. Their encouraging comments and helpful suggestions enabled me to do better work than I otherwise would have been able to do.

Much of the research for this book was done at the Disciples Historical Society in Nashville, Tennessee. The staff was consistently helpful as I had them repeatedly return to the archives to retrieve materials I needed for my work. I owe them my thanks. Two typists labored to make my mess of writing presentable, Paula Bernd from First Christian Church in Louisville, Kentucky, and Alice Price at Royal Palm Christian Church (Disciples of Christ) in Coral Springs, Florida. I have had the privilege of counting both of them as co-laborers and friends.

Several of the chapters of this book first appeared as essays in a somewhat different form in journals. Chapter Three was printed in *Encounter* 64 (Winter 2003); Chapter Four appeared in *Discipliana* 62 (Spring 2002); Chapter Five was included in *Encounter* 66 (Summer 2005); Chapter Six appeared in *Discipliana* 56 (Summer 1996) in a much shorter form; and Chapter Seven was printed in *Lexington Theological Quarterly* 37 (Fall 2002). I gratefully acknowledge the publishers of these periodicals.

# Introduction

I write these words during a time of war. I cannot do otherwise because there is no time that is not a time of war. Armed conflict rages in numerous places throughout the world every day of every year. Someone has defined peace as the pause between wars, but there is no pause; there is just a change of location. For individual nations, war may cease for a while but for the entire world...never. Yet because war is so unspeakably destructive – and increasingly so as the technology of violence advances – it is crucial that we consider things that make for peace and ponder the thoughts of those who advocate peace. Thus, with these things in mind, I offer you this book on Alexander Campbell's thoughts on pacifism, violence and the church's relationship to the state.

No one persuasively disputes the fact that Alexander Campbell (1788 - 1866) was the single most important influence in the American religious movement that produced the Disciples of Christ, the Church of Christ and the independent Christian church. Historian David Edwin Harrell, Jr. referred to Campbell as "the uncrowned monarch of the church" who "reigned over a turbulent and unruly kingdom."[1] While Campbell's leadership never went unquestioned, his impact was enormous. His mark on the churches that developed from the movement he helped found is deep and wide. Many of Campbell's convictions remain apparent in the life of the present day churches that trace their history back to him. The practice of open Communion celebrated weekly, believer's baptism by immersion, congregational autonomy, a high view of lay ministry, and a strong emphasis upon Christian unity are but a few of the many evidences of Campbell's continuing imprint. However, other facets of his teaching, while once widely embraced by members of these churches, are no longer a conspicuous part of the churches' teaching and practice. One such facet that is notably absent is a clear commitment to pacifism.

For over forty years Campbell shaped the Disciples and impacted others with his writings, speeches and public debates. Born in Ireland and educated at the University of Glasgow in Scotland, he arrived in America in 1809. Along with his father, Thomas Campbell, Alexander led a reform movement that rejected creeds and emphasized primitive Christianity. He was a Presbyterian who affiliated with Baptists for a short period of time before taking his reform movement independent. Later the churches that looked to him for leadership joined forces with a somewhat similar movement headed by Barton Stone, also a pacifist. Campbell deplored the fragmentation of the church into competing denominations and sects. Likewise, he found the hostile diversions and warring madness of nations repugnant. He called upon Christians to refuse to take up arms and instead follow the nonviolence taught in the New Testament.

Campbell lived, as we do, in a time when the overwhelming majority of Christians believed that war, while tragic, is inevitable and that Christians are obligated to fight on behalf of the nation in which they reside. Explicit affirmation of the permissibility and even the responsibility of Christians to participate in wars was given confessional status in several traditions. For instance, it is stated within the Augsburg Confession (1530) that "it is taught among us... that Christians may without sin...punish evildoers with the sword, engage in just wars, [and] serve as solders."[2] Likewise, one of the Church of England's Thirty-nine Articles (1571) reads, " It is lawful for Christian men, at the commandment of the Magistrate, to weare weapons and serve in the warres."[3] The Westminister Confession (1646), the foundational doctrinal statement of Campbell's own Presbyterian heritage, speaking of Christian magistrates, states that they "may lawfully, now under the New Testament, wage war upon just as necessary occasion."[4]

In rejecting creeds and confessions for – among other reasons – their tendency to discourage deeper study in scriptural truth, and hinder reformation, Campbell re-approached the topic of war. He found the traditional sanctions for war offered by churches as unbiblical, utterly contrary to the example and teachings of Jesus and detrimental to the nature of the church. Among the first generation of those in the religious movement he helped found – which he preferred to call Disciples of Christ[5] – virtually all who committed their views to print opposed the participation of Christians in warfare. In the writings of the early Disciples, it was support of war, rather than opposition to it, that was exceptional. While this began to change in the years immediately before the Civil War, it is noteworthy that prior to 1914, the only branch of America Protestantism – beyond the historic peace churches – to recognize pacifism as a legitimate option for its members was the Disciples of Christ.[6]

The churches whose roots are sunk in the ground cultivated by Alexander Campbell did not depart from his pacifist thought as a result of biblical and theological reflection, but rather they did so as a result of social pressures and political dynamics. His peaceable views were not refuted but rather out-shouted by those who raised their loud and impassioned voices for the so-called "necessity" of war. As Chris Hedges has recently observed, war has a way of compelling a people to think nothing else is nearly so important and to believe that the highest cause is defended and the greatest meaning is found in the midst of the deadly conflicts.[7] War incites, focuses and invigorates as nothing else seems to do, even as it destroys truth, beauty, culture and lives. In the 1860's Disciples, like Presbyterians, Methodists, Baptists, Episcopalians and others were swept away by the tsunami called war. Unlike these other groups, Disciples had pacifist leaders at the earliest point in the history of the church. Yet, unlike Anabaptist churches, Disciples did not have generations in which to solidify their peaceable position. Neither had they accumulated stories of sacrifices to undergird and exemplify pacifist convictions. Stories can deepen commitments in ways theological claims often cannot. So when war came, the majority of Disciples were unprepared to resist. After the war, most Disciples apparently forgot the anti-war position advocated by Campbell and other leaders in his movement.

There are undoubtedly other reasons Disciple churches failed to remain faithfully committed to nonviolence. One contributing factor may have been that while Campbell spoke up in opposition to Christian participation in warfare throughout his career, he did not address the matter with the frequency he did with other issues – e.g., baptism. When it was brought to his attention that some of the readers of his journal *Millennial Harbinger* weren't aware of his position, he expressed frustration. However, he refused to accept responsibility for their ignorance, blaming them instead. At one point he suggested that their failure to know and embrace his position on war was due to willful resistance or an incapacity to be taught.[8] Campbell seemed to expect the positions he advocated to be widely known if not shared, even if he did not express them with great regularity. Yet the failure to address more frequently the question of war and Christian pacifism possibly contributed to the Disciples drifting from his teaching in this area.

Not only was frequency a problem, but timing was as well. On at least one occasion Campbell proved to be less prone to teach on resisting war precisely when his message would have been most relevant. He was more ready to write or speak on war when it was not a pressing issue for the nation. His decision in this matter arose from a desire to not be seen as partisan; Campbell did not want his biblical and theological reasons for his opposition to war to be confused with the political rationale offered against war during the time of the crisis. He saw the political posturing to be divisive, so he would sometimes mute his opposition to war for the sake of church unity.

This strategy did not always leave Campbell with a clean conscience. He was not a man of many regrets, but one of his few expressions of regret took place shortly after the Mexican-American War. He declared he was "ashamed" that he had not expressed more fully his opposition to war and support for nonviolence just prior to the outbreak of hostilities. He admitted that he changed his plans to write a series of studies on war and peace because political discussions of the time turned the matter into a "party question." Not wanting to contribute to the divisiveness in the nation, he "finally determined not to touch the subject till the war was over." However, reflecting on that decision a couple years later, Campbell said he was "very sorry indeed" that he failed to address the war question and call for Christian resistance while the Mexican-American War was being fought because he "might have saved the lives of some."[9] But not only might it have saved the lives of some, Campbell would likely have had the attentive ears of many more than he would have had during times of relative calm. By not speaking out forcefully against war during a time of war, he missed an opportunity to deepen the Disciples' understanding of and commitment to pacifism precisely when it was needed most.

C. Leonard Allen has suggested that Campbell's pacifism conveyed "a narrow and privatized ethic or understanding of Christian discipleship."[10] Rather than emphasizing communal aspects of church life, Campbell stressed right doctrine and structuring of the church. The "ancient order" he sought to restore was not first of all a way of living as church but a way of being organized as church. Structural and doctrinal distinctiveness were given priority over ethical distinctiveness. Consequently, there was no pronounced call to nonconformity issued by Campbell. While he could be critical of political life in America, for the most part he maintained an optimism about American ideals and practices. Though he was a pacifist, he seemed not to perceive many deep and pervasive national values that required a counter-cultural posture on the part of the church. He largely expected Christians to be able to live within society without significant jars and clashes with the prevailing norms. He did little to cultivate a sense of displacement and otherness among Christians in America.

Apparently, discipleship and common decency at times were hard to distinguish in Campbell's mind. Consequently, as Allen pointed out, when a preacher in 1859 maintained that in order to follow Christ, Christians must "take up their crosses and bear them," Campbell answered, "There is now no cross under our government. In other words there is no persecution in our country... Hence no man in the United States has to carry a cross for Christ's sake."[11] It is only fair to note that five years later, during the turmoil of war, Campbell sounded a different note, one that called for resistance: "The times are full of corruption, and the church is contaminated with the times. We all need to be reminded in tones of tenderness, coming from the world-rending agonies of the cross, that we, people of the living God are not of the world."[12]

By this time, however, patterns of accommodation were not to be reversed quickly. A corporate habit of standing against the cultural status quo had not been formed. Campbell and the early Disciples had not fostered a consciousness of living in a society whose values – and not just generally acknowledged vices – were at odds with faithfulness. Consequently, when a time of crisis arose, the church did not rise to the occasion to practice peace when others went to war. Rather Disciples readily followed the well-worn path to the battlefield that was being taken by the vast majority. The church Campbell helped found and nurture failed to sufficiently see itself as a distinctive people, strangers and sojourners, at odds with the nation and world in which it was found. Without a clear sense of being a transforming, nonconforming people, Disciples failed to develop the communal character necessary to continue embodying the pacifism Campbell had advocated.

There are undoubtedly other reasons why the Disciples churches did not continue to be pacifist in character and conviction. According to the nature of the reform movement of which Campbell was chief leader uniformity was unlikely. The movement was anti-creedal and allowed for individual interpretations of scripture. Further, the churches of the movement were congregationally governed, not structured in a way that would be conducive to fostering the uniformity of beliefs. It has been suggested that Disciples did not remain a "peace church" because of Campbell's "failure to integrate this pacifism with the main body of the teachings he left as a legacy to his church."[13] I hope to show in the following chapters that this is not altogether the case. Certainly pacifism is not the hinge upon which the rest of Campbell's convictions swing, but neither is pacifism disconnected from those teachings.

Among the reasons I have written this book is the desire to correct a significant omission in the standard histories of the American peace movement. Campbell and the early Disciples are hardly mentioned – often not mentioned at all – in studies of pacifism and antiwar advocacy of the nineteenth century. Yet few of the figures most frequently discussed as antebellum pacifists have continued to be so influential as Alexander Campbell. He deserves a more prominent place in the history of peace movements. In the following chapters, I will attempt to indicate Campbell's place within the spectrum of viewpoints found in the peace movement during his time. He was no isolated pacifist but was knowledgeable of and influenced by the ongoing discussions and activities of contemporary peace advocates. While Campbell did not hold any leadership positions in a major peace organization, he was the most well-known and formative figure in a major religious movement, and he believed the church itself to be a peace society. Campbell is certainly worthy of the attention of any who would study American peace movements.

My second, and perhaps, more important reason for writing this book is to address the amnesia among those who in some fashion share in the religious heritage Alexander Campbell so profoundly shaped. The pacifist past of the Christian Church (Disciples of Christ), the Church of Christ and the independent Christian church has been entirely forgotten by most of the members and even many of the ministers that serve these bodies. I was struck by this fact back in the mid-1980's – during a time of arms buildup and conflict in Central America – when I was preaching on some themes that related to peace and nonviolence. A long time elder of the congregation I was serving confronted me and declared, "This sort of thing is not a part of what our church is about!"

In fact, it was, and I contend, should also be in the present. I believe the memory of the church's pacifist past should not be suppressed but rather be brought to the surface. If some choose to reject it for themselves, let them do so without claiming it is not a legitimate part of who we are as churches that grew from the reform movement of which the pacifist Alexander Campbell was at the forefront. The commitment of Campbell to restore primitive Christianity included a commitment to the primitive church's practice of nonviolent love that leaves no room for war. Those who share his commitment to be truly biblical and genuinely faithful in life and thought cannot help but benefit from learning what Campbell taught about pacifism and violence.

## Notes

1. David Edwin Harrell, Jr., *Quest for a Christian America: The Disciples of Christ and American Society to 1866* (Nashville: Disciples of Christ Historical Society, 1966), 20.
2. John H. Leith, ed., *Creeds of the Churches: A Reader in Christian Doctrine from the Present*, rev. ed., (Richmond, VA: John Knox Press, 1973), 72.
3. ibid., 280.
4. ibid., 220.
5. "Disciples of Christ" or simply "Disciples" as used in this study is meant to include the Christian Church (Disciples of Christ), the Church of Christ and the Independent Christian Church.
6. Peter Brock, *Freedom from War: Nonsectarian Pacifism 1814 - 1914* (Toronto: University of Toronto Press, 1991), 136ff.
7. Chris Hedges, *War Is A Force That Gives Us Meaning* (New York: Public Affairs, 2002).
8. Alexander Campbell, *Millennial Harbinger* (1846), 473.
9. ibid., (1848), 385.
10. C. Leonard Allen, "Testing the Metal of Pacifism" in Theron F. Schlabach and Richard T. Hughes, eds., *Proclaim Peace: Christian Pacifism from Unexpected Quarters* (Urbana, IL: University of Illinois Press, 1997), 131.
11. *Millennial Harbinger* (1859), 436 - 437.
12. *Millennial Harbinger* (1864), 4.
13. Peter Brock, *Pacifism in the United States: From the Colonial Era to the First World War* (Princeton: Princeton University Press, 1968), 422.

# Chapter 1

# Influences in Campbell's Pacifism

In the introductory essay of the inaugural issue of *The Christian Baptist*, the first journal he edited, Alexander Campbell took aim at the corruptions of Christianity that he intended to attack. Prominent among these was the church's participation in war. He took his readers on an imaginary tour of Christendom, in which he ushered them before what he believed to be shameful excesses and perversions of faith. He focused their attention on what he regarded to be the absurdity of Christians in warfare. With scornful irony, Campbell wrote, "And stranger still, see that Christian general, with his ten thousand soldiers, and his chaplain at his elbow, preaching, as he says, the gospel of goodwill among men; and hear him exhort his general and his Christian warriors to go forth with the Bible in one hand and the sword in the other, to fight the battles of God and their country; praying that the Lord would cause them to fight valiantly, and render their efforts successful in making as many widows and orphans as will afford sufficient opportunity for others to manifest the purity of their religion by taking care of them."[1] After heaping ridicule upon what he saw as deplorable corruptions of Christianity, Campbell concluded his essay citing words of scripture, "Now from these turn away."[2]

In the years that followed, Campbell continued to denounce the practice of war as incompatible with Christian faith. Upon hearing of the beginning of the Civil War, the elderly Campbell poured out in writing his grief and moral disgust at the willingness of North and South to slaughter and destroy, all the while claiming to be shaped and motivated by Christian faith. He condemned the war as a monstrosity, which "caps the climax of human folly and gratuitous wickedness."[3] He mourned that the supposedly civilized America, which boasted of its Christian origin and national mission, could stoop to clashing swords and firing cannons, spilling fraternal blood and contradicting the grand vision of national righteousness which was shared by many Americans.

Just a few years later, in 1864, Campbell ended his career as a religious journalist as he began it, by condemning Christian complicity in warfare. In the preface to the same issue in which he announced his resignation as editor of *The Millennial Harbinger*, Campbell wrote passionately of his distress over the war-torn nation and strife-ridden church. Speaking of the effects of the war on the religious movement he helped found, he wrote, "Many seem to have passed, we trust but for a time, under the 'power of the world,' and to have forgotten the spirit and service of the gospel...Brethren, we are in the midst of appalling tokens of this very defection – and who is faithful and fearless!"[4]

As noted earlier, Campbell's pacifist convictions were widely shared by early Disciples. Many of the best-known Disciples leaders were pacifists.[5] These include his father, Thomas Campbell, Barton Stone, Jacob Creath, Benjamin Franklin, Raccoon John Smith, Phillip Fall, Robert Richardson, Tolbert Fanning, Moses Lard, J.W. McGarvey and others. Certainly pacifism was not universally embraced, but most among Disciples who addressed the question of war during Campbell's lifetime were of a pacifist persuasion.[6]

It has been observed that Campbell's "thought shows striking similarities to the classical left-wing Protestantism of the sixteenth century."[7] However, Campbell denied being influenced by the Anabaptists.[8] The factors that helped shape Campbell's pacifism came from other quarters. Prominent among these were his Seceder Presbyterian Church background, American and English peace advocates, and, most important, the Bible.

## Seceder Presbyterianism

Alexander Campbell and his father Thomas were Irish Protestants. The Presbyterianism of Ireland had been imported from Scotland, and with it came a variety of sectarian disputes, which repeatedly fractured the church. The Campbells were Old Light Anti-Burgher Seceder Presbyterians. This sect was highly skeptical of any alignment of the church with the state and thus it provided fertile soil in which the seeds of Campbell's pacifism could germinate.

The Presbyterian Church became the national church in Scotland in 1690. At that time, the prevailing practice was for the lay leaders of local congregations to call the ministers who were to serve as pastors. However, in

1712, the Assembly attempted to enforce patronage laws, which would effectively deprive congregations of their ability to select their own pastors by investing lay landlords with the power to appoint ministers. This was contrary to the first *Book of Discipline* accepted by the early Scottish Reformers. Generally, the ministers appointed by the patrons were of a more progressive variety, comfortable with the "worldliness" of the elite and friendly to unorthodox thought.[9] Several dissenting ministers "formally seceded from the prevailing party...in the year 1733, and ... became the nucleus of a new party called Seceders."[10]

In 1747 another division occurred: the Seceder Presbyterians split over the question of whether certain oaths being required by the burgesses of towns, binding people to support "the religion presently professed within the realm," in effect sanctioned the practices of the National Church. Some of the Seceder Presbyterians maintained the oath did little more than support Protestantism in general. Others believed that taking the oath in effect sanctioned the abuses of the established church that Seceders had always opposed. Those who found the oath contrary to their convictions were called Anti-Burghers. Those who supported the use of the oaths were labeled Burghers. At that time the established church in Ireland, where the Campbells resided, was Anglican, but there were many Presbyterians in the north of the country. Both Burghers and Anti-Burghers sent missionaries to northern Ireland and won followers. However, the evangelists brought with them issues that were of little relevance to the situation of the new converts. Nevertheless, the divisions remained in place. Both parties of the Seceders were strict in their religious life and rigid in their convictions. However, over time, the two parties adopted what Robert Richardson, a personal friend and early biographer of Alexander Campbell, called a "milder spirit of toleration."[11] Yet in 1795, another controversy arose among both Burgher and Anti-Burgher parties. This dispute centered on the power of civil magistrates in religion. Those who supported the civil magistrates were called "New Light" in contrast to the "Old Light" party who denied civil magistrates had any legitimate religious role. Archibald Bruce, a former theology professor of Alexander Campbell's father, Thomas, was the head of the "Old Light" party. It was to this party that the Campbells were affiliated.

In considering sources of Alexander Campbell's social ethics, Harold Lunger maintained that despite the irrelevance of the specifically Scottish issues in the Seceder church, Campbell was brought up in a religious fellowship which had "come into being in opposition to the principle of establishment, and in the wing of that church which went farthest in rejecting any church - state alliance."[12] While the sect of the Presbyterians of which Campbell was a member was not pacifist, its posture toward the state was conducive to pacifism inasmuch as the sect arose in reaction against the manipulation and intrusive power of the state in relation to the church.

## English and American Peace Advocates

Among the earliest influences in the development of Campbell's pacifism were writings of English Baptist Soame Jenyns. He was a controversial author and a member of the English Parliament. Jenyns strenuously objected to the abuses of religion on the part of a manipulative state. In his debate with Robert Owens, Campbell liberally quoted Jenyns on topics related to force, war and nonviolence. At one point in the discussion, Campbell spoke of the tendency of the Christian religion to motivate good behavior in the present as it prepares people to enjoy glory in the hereafter. This inclination he contrasted with an emphasis on laws and threats of punishment, both in this life and after death, by which means governing authorities coerce citizens into compliance. Campbell cited Jenyns who stated of the latter position, that it may "make us very good citizens, but will produce but tolerable Christians."[13] The state, he argued, looks to religion to be useful to its own end rather than faithful to God's end.

Campbell contended that the object of the Christian religion was not to serve the ends of worldly powers. He again quoted Jenyns who maintained that Jesus "is the only founder of a religion in the history of mankind, which is totally unconnected with all human policy and government" and because he had no desire to dominate is "totally unconducive to any world purpose whatever." In contrast to other great founders of religion, "Christ neither aimed at, nor would accept...any such power...He refused power, riches, honor, and pleasure; and courted poverty, ignominy, tortures, and death."[14]

Campbell's refusal to recognize patriotism as a virtue suitable for Christians may have been derived from Jenyns.[15] He cited him as saying, "Patriotism...directly counteracts, the extensive benevolence of this religion." Campbell further quoted Jenyns in defense of the view that a Christian is not best understood as a citizen of any particular country but as a citizen of the world: " [P]atriotism...has ever been a favorite virtue with mankind, because it conceals self-interest under the mask of public spirit, not only fr even from themselves, and gives a license to inflict wrongs and injuries, not o[illegible] with impunity, but with applause."[16]

Beginning in 1834 there is evidence in his writings of the impact the American peace movement had on Campbell. For the most part, Campbell was very critical of moral or reform societies. He complained that "in this partizan [sic] and political age it is expected that every man must join in some one of the hundred parties against the evils that afflict society."[17] He believed the church alone was God's answer to the world's evils. However, Campbell responded positively to the societies involved in the American peace crusade. On several occasions he endorsed articles published by peace organizations, advertised their journals and published reports of some of their meetings.[18]

The peace movement in the United States began in 1815. David Low Dodge and some like-minded colleagues formed the New York Peace Society. That same year Noah Worcester began the Massachusetts Peace Society. Both men based their pacifist beliefs on the Bible.

Dodge looked upon the Bible as a book of ordinances for a kingdom not of this world, somewhat as did Campbell. Dodge had been converted after reading Jonathan Edwards and he became an active Presbyterian. Though he had served in the military, his study of the scriptures, and in particular "the examples of Christ and the precepts of the Gospel," led him to believe Christians should reject all forms of violence.[19] He maintained that Christians should not cooperate with the state insofar as military duty was concerned. Further, he held that followers of Jesus should not forcibly obstruct the policies of the government. Rather they should largely withdraw from political affairs of the world.[20]

Worcester was a Unitarian Minister and was more clearly influenced by Enlightenment humanism, "less doctrinaire and more catholic" than Dodge's group.[21] He, too, had military experience, having joined the colonial army in 1776. But by the onset of the War of 1812 his convictions had so changed that he opposed the war on religious grounds. Shortly thereafter he wrote that war is "totally repugnant to the Christian Religion, and wholly unnecessary."[22] Two years later Worcester gathered with several others to form the Massachusetts Peace Society. The Society did not in the least discourage political involvement. In fact, the presidency of the organization was filled by the state governor, William Phillips. Many prominent citizens held membership in the organization.

Those who believed in the right of self-defense and "just war" were welcome as members.

Other such organizations soon proliferated in various states. In 1828 the American Peace Society united many of the diverse groups that had sprung up around the country into a loose association tolerating a variety of views. The Society was led by former sea captain William Ladd. Its ranks included members of both state and federal legislature, as well as members of the military.[23]

Of American peace advocates, it appears that none impressed Campbell more than Thomas S. Grimké. He came from a family of radical activists. His sisters, Angelina and Sarah Grimké, were strong advocates for women's equality and abolitionism. He was a Yale graduate, important plantation owner and for several years a senator in the South Carolina legislature. Grimké challenged the American Peace Society's uneasy alliance of diverse antiwar views. Upon reading a pamphlet by British Quaker Jonathan Dymond entitled *The Application of the Pacific Principles of the New Testament to the Conduct of States*, Grimké adopted an absolute pacifist stance. His change of conviction was not widely known, however, until in 1832 when the Connecticut Peace Society – an American Peace Society affiliate – invited Grimké to deliver an address in New Haven, to which a number of state dignitaries had been invited.

His message was a vigorous, uncompromising condemnation of war based on the Bible. Grimké declared, "War in any shape, from any motive, and carried on in any mode, is utterly indefensible on Christian principles and utterly irreconcilable with a Christian spirit." He continued, "Let the heathen take arms against each other and even against us, but come what may, Christians never will bear arms against each other or against them."[24] He went so far as to condemn the American Revolution as unchristian and unnecessary. The address led to considerable controversy within the American Peace Society and for himself personally. Yet William Ladd found Grimké's arguments compelling, as did many others in the peace movement. For a period of time, the American Peace Society adopted an absolute pacifist position to a great extent due to Grimké's influence.

In the portion of Campbell's library that has been preserved in Bethany, West Virginia there remains a copy of Grimké's New Haven address, as well as writings of Grimké's pacifist mentor, Jonathan Dymond.[25] It is noteworthy that in August, 1834 Campbell published in the *Millennial Harbinger* two sections of an address by Grimké on the function of the Bible as a textbook in schools in which points are made that were very similar to those in the New Haven speech.[26] The first was headed, "The Spirit of the Nations of Antiquity Was the Spirit of Selfishness, of Rapine, and of War." The second is titled, "Christian Scheme of Education." In the addresses, the spirit of war "that lives and moves throughout the classical models" is contrasted with the Gospel spirit which is "essentially the spirit of peace and humility, love and forbearance."[27]

There may be evidence of Grimké's influence in Campbell's stated displeasure with having a bird of prey, an eagle, as the national symbol of the United States,[28] and for the suggestion that Washington and other prominent American revolutionaries might have been able to accomplish their goals non-violently had they been better educated.[29] Grimké's mark is also left upon Campbell's most substantial anti-war work, his "An Address on War," which concludes with a citation from "the eloquent Grimké" who declares that "the great objection to war is not so much the numbers of lives and the amount of property it destroys, as its moral influence on nations and individuals."[30]

## The Place of the Bible

While Campbell occasionally acknowledged his indebtedness to other thinkers, he was more prone to assert his independence. He wrote to an uncle in 1815, "What I am in religion I am from examination, reflection, conviction, not from...tradition or human authority."[31] Campbell had little trust for creeds, official teachings or ineffable and direct instruction from the Holy Spirit to the individual mind. Campbell insisted, "God now speaks to us only by his Word. By his Son, in the New Testament, he has fully revealed himself and his will. This is the only revelation of his spirit we are to regard."[32] Throughout his life, Campbell held, "Veneration for the Word of God, and trembling regard for it, is a principle of action."[33]

He taught that while all scripture is inspired of God, not all scripture is equally authoritative for Christians. Campbell asserted that in order to understand and apply any portion of scripture one must be attentive to the dispensation to which it properly pertains.[34] He believed history to be divided into three ages or dispensations: the Patriarchal dispensation continued from Adam to Moses; the Jewish dispensation from Moses to Christ; and the Christian dispensation from the Resurrection of Christ to endless eternity.[35] He believed that during the first dispensation God spoke directly with the patriarchs to guide and inform them. During this period the people depended upon traditions that were passed on from generation to generation.[36]

The second dispensation began after the Ten Commandments were given to Moses, and were elaborated and codified in the Old Testament. These laws were not for all people or for all time, according to Campbell. They were revealed specifically for the Jewish people to be used during that period before Jesus ascended to be Lord and King. The laws contained in the Old Testament were given to guide the chosen nation of Israel that it might be faithful to the truth of God and prepare both itself and the world for the promised Christ.

According to Campbell, after Jesus was crucified, raised and crowned King of kings, God instituted a change of rituals and laws. He insisted that Christians should not look to the Old Testament for authority for the practices of the church. Just as the Jews were not to look to the patriarchal age for commands, "neither are the statutes and laws of the Christian kingdom to be sought for in the Jewish scripture, not antecedent to the day of Pentecost, except so far as our Lord himself, during his life-time, propounded the doctrine of his reign.[37]

Only the authority of Christ and the apostles was definitive for the church according to Campbell. He held that Christians were not to be ruled by a system of laws, but guided by the principle of love. "Laws expressed in words," he wrote, "assail the ears and aim at restraining actions; but love pierces to the heart, and disarms the rising thought of mischievous intent."[38] While Campbell did not deny there were lessons to be learned from the Old Testament, it was only in the New Testament that Christians could receive the guidance needed to properly order the church and faithfully live life under the Lordship of Jesus Christ.[39]

Given the dispensational principles of interpretation Campbell embraced, participation in war could not be justified by appealing to examples within the Old Testament. He did not believe the God-directed wars of the Jewish age were immoral, but neither were they precedent-setting for Christians. Campbell held that God used the nation of Israel "to execute the judgments he had decreed against their heathen assailants, spoilers, and depredators."[40] He contended: "wars waged by God's people in their typical character, were waged under and in pursuance of a special divine commission. They were, therefore, right."[41] Still, however right the wars of the Jewish age may have been, they have no bearing on Christians. Only a direct command from God could justify Christian involvement in warfare and such a command would not be given, held Campbell. Jesus Christ alone has the right to set the standards of behavior for Christians and his law is love.

Campbell was aware of the writings of some who sought to make a case for Christian participation in war by appeals to the Old Testament. Books that made such attempts were viewed by him as abusive of scripture. His view was that such "volumes to this effect only convince me of the ignorance of some and the hypocrisy of others, from whose reputation for candor, intelligence, and piety we might have expected better things."[42] For Campbell only those convictions that can be rooted in the New Testament count as genuinely Christian.

He held that those who sought to define Christian behavior by appeals to the Old Testament find themselves inadvertently defending more than they intend. "We can justify many of the Old Testament wars on as good and relevant grounds as we justify polygamy, divorce and certain forms of slavery, because there was no separate and spiritual community erected on earth from Adam to the last Pentecost,"[43] wrote Campbell. In his view the church now exists to be that separate and spiritual community, a people living under the New Covenant and guided by Jesus Christ who has "all authority in heaven and earth."[44]

This hermeneutical approach does not mean that Campbell entirely ignored the Old Testament as he built his case for pacifism. He repeatedly referred to the messianic title "Prince of Peace" (Isa. 9:6).[45] He also cited the prophesies regarding the coming age in which weapons of war will be transformed into instruments of production and peace (Isa. 2: 2-4; Micah 4: 3-4).[46] When discussing the origins of war, Campbell alludes to two Old Testament passages. The first passage pertains to the mythic war in heaven and subsequent expulsion of Lucifer (Isa. 14: 12ff). The second passage is the temptation and fall narrative (Gen. 3: 1ff).[47] But aside from these few references, the Old Testament was given slight attention.

Campbell drew heavily from the book of Acts and the Epistles of Paul when dealing with most of the subjects that occupied his attention. This was not the case in his writings on war and peace. Still, he did occasionally cite Paul. Most often he pointed to Ephesians 6:10ff in which Paul asserts that the warfare of Christians is spiritual and not material and the equipment needed are qualities of character and conviction rather than literal military articles and tools of violence. Campbell also pointed to Romans 12: 14ff which calls for a repudiation of seeking vengeance, renounces returning evil for evil and calls upon Christians to practice peace toward others to the fullest extent of their ability.[48] He drew from a single passage in the book of James ( 4:1-3) when addressing the source of wars.[49]

The great majority of biblical passages from which Campbell drew came from the Gospels. He quoted the angelic words found in the nativity story to indicate the character of the ministry of Christ: "peace on earth and good will amongst men" (Lk. 2:14),[50] which he understood as leaving no room for Christians to practice violence or engage in war. Campbell also cited two incidences from the night of Jesus' betrayal. The first was Peter's attempt to defend Jesus by force of arms in which Jesus chastised him, demanding that he put away the weapon "for those who live by the sword shall die by the sword" (Matt. 26: 51f). Campbell also repeatedly referenced Jesus' statement to Pilate, "If my kingdom were of this world my servants would fight, but my kingdom is not of this world"(John 18:36).[51] He saw Jesus teaching in these words that war would be justifiable for disciples if and only if Christ's kingdom was visible, tangible and geographical. Since Jesus himself taught this was not the case, Christians certainly cannot fight for other realms. This will be discussed further in the next chapter.

Among the Gospel references used by Campbell, many came from the Sermon on the Mount. He claimed, "The sermon on the mount is an exponent of the Savior's mind and will on the subject of war. If he would not have any of them to render evil for evil, and if he pronounced the highest honor and blessing on the peace-makers, who can imagine that he could be the patron of war!"[52] Campbell quoted Jesus' beatitude upon those who make peace and noted the lack of a similar blessing bestowed upon conquerors, heroes and patriots. He pointed to Jesus' command to "turn the other cheek" and to "love your enemies" and called upon all to submit to the kind and trustworthy authority of Jesus rather than practice reprisal or strike out with violence.[53]

Campbell's dispensational hermeneutic is not unique to himself. David Low Dodge was the first American peace reformer who argued against those who appealed to the Old Testament to justify the practice of war by contending that Christians live under a different dispensation. The Old Testament period was preparatory and temporary, paving the way for Jesus Christ. Though God had permitted holy wars in times past, the gospel of peace supercedes all earlier commands and standards of behavior. As animal sacrifices had been abolished and replaced by the all-sufficient Christ, so too had earthly, literal warfare been replaced by spiritual warfare fought with spiritual weapons. No longer did God command the army of any nation to exact divine vengeance. Rather, Christ commanded his followers to love their enemies. In view of the change of dispensations, Dodge concluded, "It is sinful to exercise any affection toward enemies short of that benevolence or mercy that invokes the advancement of their best good."[54] Campbell was in full agreement.

Clearly the Bible, interpreted through the lens of his dispensationalism, was the most significant influence in the formulation of Campbell's pacifism. But the Bible was not the only factor in shaping his thoughts. The Seceder Presbyterianism with its suspicion of the manipulative power of the state in relation to the church helped set the stage for his thinking. Further, writings of contemporary advocates of nonviolence such as Jenyns, Grimké, Dymond and others impressed him. So it was not only while isolated in personal biblical study that his pacifist views developed but in conversation with his times.

## Notes

1. *Christian Baptist*, I, (Bethany, Virginia, 1823), 17-18.
2. ibid.
3. *Millennial Harbinger*, (Bethany, Virginia, 1861), 348.
4. *Millennial Harbinger*, (1864), 3f.
5. Winfred Ernest Garrison and Alfred T. DeGroot, *The Disciples of Christ: A History* (St. Louis: Christian Board of Publication, 1948), 335.
6. Harrell, 139ff.
7. Harold L. Lunger, *The Political Ethics of Alexander Campbell* (St. Louis: Bethany Press, 1954), 18.
8. Alexander Campbell and N.L. Rice, *A Debate on the Action, Subject, Design and Administration of Christian Baptism: Also, on the Character of Spiritual Influence in Conversion and Sanctification, and on the Expediency and Tendency of Ecclesiastical Creeds, as Terms of Union and Communion* (Lexington, KY: A.T. Skillman & Son, 1844) 873.
9. George Richard Phillips, "Differences in the Theological and Philosophical Background of Alexander Campbell and Barton W. Stone and the Resulting Differences in Their Theological Formation, " Ph.D. dissertation, Vanderbilt University, 1968, 129.

10. Robert Richardson, *The Memoirs of Alexander Campbell*, I (Philadelphia: J.B. Lippencott & Co., 1868), 53. This volume provides the chief source of information on Thomas and Alexander Campbell prior to their arrival in America. All of this section is dependent upon Richardson unless otherwise noted.
11. ibid., 55.
12. Lunger, 20.
13. Alexander Campbell and Robert Owen, *The Evidences of Christianity: A Debate* (Philadelphia: James Challen & Son, 1863), 406.
14. ibid., 407.
15. Alexander Campbell, *Popular Lectures and Addresses* (James Challen & Son: Philadelphia, 1864), 184.
16. *The Evidences of Christianity: A Debate*, 409.
17. *Millennial Harbinger*, (1836), 282.
18. ibid., 1834, 306f, 1839, 96; 1840, 458, 480, *The Christian Baptist*, IV, 143.
19. Cited in Valarie H. Ziegler, *The Advocates of Peace in Antebellum America* (Bloomington: Indiana University Press, 1992), 22-23.
20. Charles Chatfield, "The Bible and American Peace Movements" in *The Bible and Social Reform*, ed. Ernest R. Sandern (Fortress Press: Philadelphia, 1982), 106.
21. Merle Eugene Curti, *The American Peace Crusade 1815 - 1860* (Durham, N.C.: Duke University Press, 1929), 11.
22. Ziegler, 23.
23. Peter Brock, *Pacifism in the United States: From the Colonial Era to the First World War* (Princeton, N.J.: Princeton University Press, 1968), 482ff.
24. Cited in Ziegler, 44.
25. Lunger, 246.
26. *Millennial Harbinger*, (1834), 341ff.
27. Lunger, 246.
28. ibid., 246.
29. *Millennial Harbinger*, (1841), 437.
30. *Millennial Harbinger*, (1848), 385.
31. Cited in Richardson, I, 466.
32. *The Christian Baptist*, (1823), 188.
33. *Millennial Harbinger*, (1830), 423.
34. Alexander Campbell, *The Christian System* (Gospel Advocates: Nashville, 1969), 4.
35. Campbell's dispensationalism will be explained further in a later chapter.
36. *The Christian System*, op. cit., 121f.
37. ibid., 133.
38. *The Evidences of Christianity: A Debate*, 397.
39. *Millennial Harbinger*, (1834), 410.
40. ibid., (1846), 639.
41. *Millennial Harbinger*, (1848), 370.
42. *Millennial Harbinger*, (1846), 640.
43. ibid.

44. *Millennial Harbinger*, (1848), 370.
45. *Millennial Harbinger*, (1846), 640; (1849), 383; (1850), 524.
46. *Millennial Harbinger*, (1848), 375, 383.
47. ibid., (1846), 639f., *Millennial Harbinger*, (1861), 345f.
48. *Millennial Harbinger*, (1846), 641; (1848), 376; (1861), 338.
49. ibid., (1861), 346.
50. *Millennial Harbinger*, (1846), 641; (1850), 524.
51. ibid., (1846), 640f.
52. ibid., 641.
53. *Millennial Harbinger*, (1833), 120; (1848), 385.
54. Cited in Valarie H. Ziegler, *The Advocates of Peace in Antebellum America* (Bloomington, IN: Indiana University Press, 1992), 30.

# Chapter 2

# The Chief Characteristics of Campbell's Pacifism

Pacifism takes a variety of forms. While all of them are expressions of opposition to war and violence, they can differ in rationale, limitations and goals, among other things. Pacifism is not a single position. In this chapter we will examine some of the defining characteristics of Campbell's understanding of war and Christian nonviolence. The following chapters will explore how Campbell's pacifism relates to some other relevant facets of his thought.

## The Authority of Christ

Campbell rooted his pacifism in the authority of Jesus Christ. He insisted that any justification of war by Christians must find its warrant in the life and teaching of Christ. For Campbell, the key question was, "Has the Author and Founder of the Christian religion enacted war, or has he made it lawful and right for the subjects of his government to go to war against one another? Or has he made it right for them to go to war against any nation, for any national object, at the bidding of the present existent political authorities of any nation in Christendom?"[1]

As discussed in the previous chapter, the question of war for Campbell could not be settled by an indiscriminate appeal to the Bible since "it certainly authorized war among the Jews."[2] But that authorization does not extend to Christians. The wars waged by the Jews, as reported in the Old Testament, were a result of a divine mandate, and hence beyond criticism according to Campbell. The people of Israel existed under a theocratic government. The express command of God required the people of God to engage in the wars recorded in scripture as they conquered and then defended the land given to them by God. Such wars were "waged under and in pursuance of a special divine commission. They were, therefore, right."[3]

However, Campbell held that in the time since Christ, there has been no divine warrant for war. Any presence on the battlefield by Christians is not only without God's authorization but contrary to the command of Christ. "What the God of Abraham did by Abraham, by Jacob, or by any of his sons, as the then moral governor of the world, before he gave up the scepter and the crown to his Son Jesus Christ, is of no binding authority now." The authority of God is no longer expressed apart from, but always through, Jesus Christ. He is rightfully Lord and King on earth as in heaven. Since "all legislative, judiciary, and executive power" is now in the hands of Christ, any attempt to justify war by appealing to any other authority is misguided, according to Campbell. He challenged those who believe Christians can have a place on the battlefield to produce "a special divine warrant or right for carrying on war by the authority of the Lord Jesus Christ...the present Monarch of the universe."[4]

The fact that all authority is in the hands of Christ transforms the way governmental authority is to be viewed by Christians. Campbell maintained that at Jesus' ascension into heaven he declared all authority on heaven and earth had been given to him, hence the "Kings of the earth and courts of high judicature are all under him, but they do not really acknowledge it."[5] Consequently, followers of Christ recognize limits of civil government that governments themselves do not concede. Governments imagine themselves with the right to declare wars and compel Christians to fight in them. However, taught Campbell, because of the authority of Jesus Christ such a right does not exist. As supreme sovereign, Jesus supercedes all other authority for Christians.

Campbell held that governments have a legitimate role and authority under Christ. In most instances, Christians are to be willing and obedient subjects. To the extent that the governing powers function within the constraints of Christ's authority, they are servants of God. Yet insofar as war is concerned, Christians owe nothing to the governing authorities of any nation. "On the contrary," wrote Campbell, "they were to live peaceably with all men to the full extent of their power. Their sovereign Lord, the King of nations, is called 'THE PRINCE OF PEACE.'"[6] The commitment to nonviolence is a response above all to the authority of Jesus Christ, a point that will be discussed further in chapter six.

## Church Unity

Campbell's opposition to war was in part an expression of his abiding passion for the unity of the church. Early in his career he published an ironical "Third Epistle of Peter" in which he offered this deliberately dubious advice to ministers: "If a brother shall rise up the banner of war against brother, and Christians against Christian, rebuke them not; but be some of you on one side and some on the other; and tell the one host that God is on their side, and the other host that he is on their side: so make them bold to kill. And even among swords and lances let your black robes be seen. Preach ye not 'Peace on earth and good will to men,' but preach ye glory to the victor, and victory to the brave."[7] For Campbell, few things were viewed as more detrimental to the mission and unity of the church than war.

The primary problem of war for Campbell was not the violence of nation against nation but of the church against the church. He decried Christians and churches in different countries lining up in support of their respective governments with a willingness to kill one another in the name of God. As citizens of the kingdom of Christ, Christians betrayed their loyalty to the Prince of Peace by waging war against the Lord's subjects in other lands. The question as Campbell posed it in his "An Address on War" was, "Can Christ's kingdom or church in one nation wage war against his own kingdom or church in another nation?"[8]

In stating the question in this way he defined war, insofar as it involves Christians, not simply as an act of hostility of national powers against each other, but as a violent disruption within the church, and a disfiguration of the reign of Christ. Campbell insisted that Christians in one nation had no right to take up arms at the bidding of the government against another nation in which there were Christians. Thus, Christians participating in such a war placed the church against itself. The integrity of the church must take precedent over the interests of any nation. The loyalty Christians owe one another relativizes and limits any loyalty that may be owed to others. The integrity and unity of the church must be preserved regardless of the security interests of one's nation.

Since Christians of all nations are members of one kingdom, war is an attack on the subjects of the one rightful King Jesus Christ. No nation on earth can be rightly regarded as Christian in contrast to other nations and so claim to be fighting for God and against the ungodly. There is but "one Christian Nation, composed of all the Christian communities and individuals in the whole earth" and that nation is the church.[9] As Christians submit to their one true sovereign, they live as subjects of a not-of-this-world kingdom, which exists without regard to boundaries of nations. The allegiance that churches of differing nations owe to Christ makes any war that would set Christian against Christian an outrageous prospect. So Campbell rhetorically asks, "Is there a man of ordinary Bible education in this city or commonwealth that would, or could, affirm that Christ's church in England may of right wage war against Christ's church in America?"[10] Campbell reframes the issue of war. For Christians it can never be merely a violent contest between nations but a matter of the self-destruction of the church.

Campbell protested against the abuse of the pulpit, which takes place as ministers promote the cause of their nation in war. He held that glorifying war heroes, offering prayers for victory against enemies and perpetrating the myth of the righteousness of one's own nation ended up "desecrating the religion of the Prince of Peace by causing [the church] to minister as a handmaid of war."[11] Whenever the church lifts its voice to sanction and support a war, the saving and unifying message of the gospel is discredited. Campbell deplored the practice of elevating military heroes to a stature comparable to saints and of speaking of those who fall in battle as if they are martyrs. All such exercises align Christians in one nation with their compatriots to the exclusion of others. Instead of being an instrument of God to break down the walls of hostility between peoples, Campbell contended that too frequently the church builds the walls higher.

The objection Campbell had to the "pagan virtues" of Valor, Patriotism and Friendship was that they promote division by fostering loyalties that are too limited. Such virtues too often serve to advance the interests of one people over and against others. Consequently, Campbell saw them as contrary to Christianity because they are "too narrow and confined" and "benevolent to a single object" rather than seeking the good for all.[12] Campbell held that no "virtue" that served to benefit some to the destruction of others could be regarded as Christian. Bravery and courage, so praised by empires and nations, were not viewed by Campbell as among the high moral excellencies because they were most often enacted in violent and divisive conflict. Genuinely Christian virtues cannot be put to service in war since "we have no Christian nation or kingdom in the world; but that Christ has one grand kingdom composed of all the Christian communities in the world, of which he is himself its proper sovereign, its lawgiver and king."[13]

Campbell argued that wars among more thoroughly pagan nations were more "rational" than wars between "our miscalled Christian nations."[14] The pagans of different nations did not worship the same gods. The power of the gods was supposedly demonstrated in battle. In contrast, Christians of all nations share a single God. But in the midst of war, Christians on all sides of a conflict irrationally invoke a single God and pray for victory for themselves and the defeat of the others. The lack of a vital and resilient unity evident in such practice, claimed Campbell, does nothing to commend Christianity or honor Christ. To the contrary, Christ is discredited. The witness of the church to the world is undermined.

Because of the centrality of the church in his thinking, his understanding of pacifism was communal. For Campbell, it is not just the exceptional heroic individual who is called to nonviolence. Rather, it is the nature of the Christian community itself that demands nonviolence, not an individualist focus on moral perfectionism. He maintained that the church cannot genuinely be true to its nature if its members among the various nations fail to place the loyalty they have for Christ and one another over the responsibility they have toward their respective nations. The relationship they share because of Christ leaves no place for war. Concern for the unity of the church must take precedence over the animosity between nations insofar as Christian action is concerned.

## The Sources of War

Campbell stood against the idea that war is a legitimate means for a just authority to oppose an unjust power that oppresses the weak and deprives people of their rights. His views were directly contrary to those of contemporaries such as the Rev. George H. Corey who, speaking of the motives for the Civil War said, "We made war the instrument of justice, the herald of liberty. When the war is waged for a principle, for benign institutions, then the war-wave rolls with the impetus and weight of an idea and the energy of moral enthusiasm."[15] Campbell considered such a notion self-deceptive, spiritually hazardous and biblically ignorant. In the year the Civil War began, Campbell alluded to Romans

12:17-19, writing that "there is a wrong way of seeking our rights. The Christian is not permitted to redress his wrongs by taking vengeance upon the wrong-doer. He is to commit his cause to Him who judges righteously, to whom vengeance belongs."[16]

If violence could truly be a means of justice and God's will is confirmed in the victory of one party over another, Campbell observed, then a less wasteful and destructive means to achieve that end can be found. He proposed that nations could more wisely proceed "by selecting, each, one of their Simon Pure patriots and heroes, and having them voluntarily to meet in single combat, before a competent number of witnesses, and encountering each other till one of them triumphed; and thus award, from Heaven's own court of infallible rectitude, to the nation of the survivor, the glory of a great national triumph, both of heroism and justice."[17] But, argued Campbell, such a contest will not happen because so-called Christian nations do not truly trust in the providence and moral government of God. Victory in war goes, not to the just, but to the stronger.

According to Campbell, the Christian has no divine warrant to advance or protect the rights or interests of any individual or group if such an action "necessarily involves [taking] the lives of his fellow creatures."[18] The act of war could never arise from a spirit of righteousness. "The spirit of war is always a rebellious spirit. The authority resisted maybe just or unjust."[19] Campbell recognized no moral difference between offensive and defensive wars or just and unjust wars. He viewed such a distinction as artificial. Campbell pointed out that though all Europe considered Napoleon one of the most aggressive warriors there ever was, on his deathbed he claimed he had never engaged in an aggressive war. Thus the distinction between wars is useless, "for a mere grammatical, logical or legal quibble will make any war either aggressive or defensive, just as the whim, caprice or interest of an individual please."[20]

Campbell confessed that the historical causes of wars are not easily discerned and too frequently masked by rhetoric. If the true originating causes were fairly considered, wars would probably lack the motivational power to inspire the courage and determination of the conscientious soldier.[21] Campbell cited a study done some years earlier by the Peace Society of Massachusetts of 286 wars of notable size, from the time of Constantine the Great until the early nineteenth century. Not one war was for defense alone.[22] The outcome of the wars did not reveal which party in the conflict was right, nor punish the more guilty, or further the rights of the innocent, according to Campbell. "War is not now, nor was it ever, a process of justice. It never was a test of truth – a criterion of right. It is either a mere game of chance, or a violent outrage of the strong upon the weak."[23]

If the source of war is not found in an unavoidable encounter between the guilty aggressor and the innocent defender, what is the source of wars? Campbell looked to the New Testament for his answer. Citing the Epistle of James, he replied, "From whence come wars and fighting among you? Come they not hence - even of your lusts, that war in your members? You lust and have not, you kill and desire to have, and cannot obtain: you fight and war, yet you have not, because you ask not. You ask and receive not, because you ask amiss, that you may consume it upon your lusts."[24] Campbell understood the source of war as being the passion to possess, institutionalized in the political life of nations. Historical causes were secondary to Campbell, merely overt and diverse expressions of an under-laying evil. "Cupidity, the desire to have, without a just and indefensible right, what belongs to a neighbor, and hatred toward the other party when seeking redress of injury, are the usual provocatives of the war spirit."[25]

## Not-of-this-World Kingdom

In Campbell's writings on war and peace no words of scripture are cited more often than Jesus' statement to Pilate, "My kingdom is not of this world. If my kingdom were of this world, my servants would have fought that I should not be delivered to the Jews. But now is my kingdom not from hence." (John 18:36)[26] For Campbell, this passage alone was sufficient reason to restrict Christians from the battlefield. If the cause of Jesus Christ could not be defended by force of arms surely no lesser cause can impel Christians to fight. Only if Christ's kingdom were worldly with territory and borders that needed to be defended would there be justification for Christians to take up arms.

Campbell understood the principles upon which Christ's kingdom is established to be equity, peace and love. Consequently, there could be no room for revenge on the part of either individuals or nations.[27] When loyalty to Christ's kingdom is not supreme, Campbell wrote, "Men... can eloquently, convincingly, and persuasively explain away any precept of the law or of the gospel."[28] He noted that it had been argued by others that Jesus intended, not to forbid warfare, but to stop his followers from fighting for him because he was destined by God to die as a sin offering. Campbell countered that such a position fails to recognize the reason Jesus himself gave for refusing to allow his disciples to fight. It had nothing to do with the need for a sin offering. Rather the reason that the disciples were not to fight was because fighting was out of keeping with the nature of his kingdom. "If, then," asked Campbell, "the Messiah would not, in defense of his own life, have his servants to take the sword, for whose life ought it to be unsheathed?"[29] The fighting appropriate for Christians is not earthly and carnal, but spiritual. Campbell quoted the apostle Paul in defense of this position: "The weapons of our warfare are not carnal but spiritual. We wrestle not with flesh and blood, but with the rulers of the darkness of this world, with wicked spirits in the regions of the air." (Eph. 6:12)[30]

The weapons suitable for the not-of-this-world kingdom are not of much use on a battlefield of this world, Campbell observed. He contrasted the equipment of the soldier loyal to Christ's kingdom with those who live and die by the sword. Campbell asked, "How then could a Christian soldier, whose 'shield' was faith, whose 'helmet' was the hope of salvation, whose 'breastplate' was righteousness, whose 'girdle' was truth, whose 'feet were shod with the preparation of the gospel of peace,' and whose 'sword' was that fabricated by the Holy Spirit, even 'the Word of God,' – I say, how could such a one enlist to fight the battles of a Caesar, a Hannibal, a Tamerlane, a Napoleon, or even a Victoria?"[31] The "equipment" the Christians need for spiritual warfare render them of little use for the battle fought by the nations.

Campbell mentions "dull scholars" who sought to justify Christians in warfare by citing the statement Jesus made shortly before his betrayal to his yet unprepared disciples: "You had better sell your outside garments and buy a sword" (Luke 22:36). Campbell maintained the words figuratively indicate the trials to come and the need to be spiritually prepared. He noted that one of the disciples took Jesus' words literally, "as some friends of war still do." That disciple replied, "Lord, here are two swords" (Luke 22:38). Clearly, two swords for twelve disciples were not going to help much in a fight. But, Campbell contended, Jesus had no intention of having disciples to fight with swords. "It is enough," said Jesus because, according to Campbell, "his kingdom neither came nor stands by the sword."[32] The kingdom to come would be a realm without weapons.

The nature of Christ's reign was foretold in prophesy, said Campbell. Quoting the well-known words of Isaiah: "He shall judge among the nations, and decide among many people. And they shall beat their swords to ploughshares, and their spears into pruning-hooks; nations shall not lift up sword against nation, neither shall they learn war anymore," (Isa. 2:4) and the similarly worded passage in Micah 4:3, Campbell stated, "Decidedly, then, the spirit of Christianity is essentially pacific."[33] He believed followers of Jesus should live as a people who are most deeply invested in a realm beyond that accessible to the senses but which deeply impacts the world for those who have faith.

## Humanitarian Concern

Campbell's pacifism was justified not just by theological and biblical principles, but also by rational and humanitarian argument. Indeed, S. Morris Eames claimed, "On such social matters as war and capital punishment ... he did some Biblical searching, but his views emerge more as an outcome of his philosophy of the Enlightenment than of Biblical pronouncements."[34] This assertion, I believe, is an overstatement. However, it is clear that Campbell's opposition to war is not rooted solely in scripture. Reasons independent of his distinctly Christian convictions undergird his pacifism. In fact, near the conclusion of his "An Address On War," he declared that "were I not a Christian ... I would plead this cause" against war.[35] Campbell believed that much of the evidence against war was of such a nature as to be compelling to any rational person.

He did not hesitate to marshal arguments against war that would appeal to a person without faith. Writing of the war with Mexico, he lamented the loss of 40,000 lives and the expenditure of nearly $150,000,000 that could have been put to more constructive use. In addition, Campbell reminded his readers that the war left countless widows and orphans, many of whom were desperately impoverished and in need of the support of the resource limited community. "Their tears, and agonies, and misfortunes, no numbers can tell."[36] He noted that the population crucial for the growing country was diminished by war. The men who returned from the battlefields frequently were demoralized and broken. War, wrote Campbell, "works mischief and ruin in all directions, and blunts or paralyzes the noblest and best feelings of the human heart.[37]

Campbell expressed similar concerns at the beginning of his "An Address on War." He spoke of the "desolations and horrors of war," the grief of the families who had relatives killed in battle, and the needless property loss of nations and individuals. Drawing from the calculations of other researchers, he estimated the loss of lives from wars through the centuries in the hundreds of millions."[38] The wealth spent in the support of the armies who butchered those millions is, he wrote, "a sum much more easily expressed than comprehended by even the most accomplished financier."[39] But more important, considering the great dignity and high value to be found in each individual human life according to the Christian revelation, "how insignificant are the temporary and passing results of any course of [military] action, compared with those which know neither measure nor end!"[40]

Campbell believed that war leads not just to needless death, suffering and destruction but to moral degradation. "I think that moral desolations of war surpass even its horrors," he wrote.[41] As bad as the inhumane and destructive behavior of men in war can be, Campbell saw other moral fatalities. War is a "contagion" that produces the "corruption of public taste." The deceptive glory of war captivates women – mothers, sisters, relatives – who honor the warriors and admire the trappings of the military. They are distracted from nobler life-enhancing pursuits of art, education and compassion in order to contribute to the war effort.[42] The war spirit also corrupts the nurture and education of the young, claimed Campbell: "Behold, too, the young mother arraying her proud boy 'with cap and feather, toyed with a drum and sword,' training him for the admired profession of a man-killer!"[43] In schools, students are led to misdirect their praise by being taught to look to warriors as role models rather than instructed that those most worthy of honor resolve conflicts without resorting to violence.

Even in churches military heroes are celebrated and honored, protested Campbell. He took this to be a sign of the corrosive influence of the war spirit that eats away at the vision and virtue that is necessary for spiritual and moral health. Speaking of works of art in churches, he complained that, not only in Europe, but in the United States as well, "we find St. Paul driven out of the church to make room for generals and commodores renowned in fight."[44] Statues are erected and high praise is given for those who "gloriously fell" while trying to kill for their country. Campbell found it particularly repugnant that churches would rejoice that God caused thousands of their enemies to be destroyed, creating multitudes of widows and orphans.[45] All of this appalled Campbell who insistently proclaimed, "War and Christianity are Antipodal."[46]

## Optimism

Campbell's pacifism was undergirded with an optimistic vision of the future. He was convinced that moral, spiritual and intellectual progress were willed by God and inevitable for humankind. The postmillennial theology embraced by Campbell fit well with the Enlightenment confidence in progress, which he and many of his contemporaries had absorbed. While he believed that the church, the academy and the nations had taken many missteps that needed correction, he still had great confidence in the overall direction of history. Campbell trusted that along with a restored church, the human mind and institutions had the capacity to pave the way for the peaceable kingdom.

The optimism of Campbell stands in stark contrast to the theological pessimism that was occasionally voiced in his time. This is evident in an exchange Campbell had with Samuel M. McCorkle in the mid-1830's. McCorkle held that human effort could do nothing to usher in Christ's second coming. Christ will reign on earth by divine action only: "Man is never consulted relative to these matters, it is always the work of God. He alone can repeal or change the administration of his moral government on earth."[47] No amount of activity or education would be sufficient to adequately prepare the world for Christ. McCorkle held that "the present cannot be renovated."[48] In the past, he contended, corrupt human legislation misgoverned the world and the future will bring more of the same. "It is quite absurd to expect moral perfection, which holy writ warrants us to look for during Christ's universal reign, to rise out of the present dispensation," McCorkle concluded.[49] To him the promises of progress were deceptive and empty.

Campbell thought otherwise. Under the pseudonym "A Reformed Clergyman," Campbell wrote, "Compare Christendom in the year 1834, with Christendom in the year 1534 ... Has there been no retrograde motion during these three centuries?"[50] He named Bacon, Locke and Newton as innovators who have moved the world forward in politics, economics, physical science and morals. Luther, Calvin, Zwingli and others opened the door of freedom in the church. The printing press made it easier to confront error and spread the truth. The creative powers of the nineteenth century outstripped those of previous ages. The overthrow of evil, believed Campbell, was "gradual and progressive," God working through human agency rather than apart from it.[51]

This optimistic confidence in progress is evident in his decision to publish an excerpt from an address presented to the Congress of the Friends of Universal

Peace. It was delivered by the organization's president, M.V. Hugo, on August 24, 1849. Campbell commends it as an "elegant and sensible address ... characterized by remarkable eloquence and lofty sentiment."[52]

Many of the themes found in Campbell's writings are present in the paper. "Look at the vast number of discoveries which [God] causes to be made by human genius, and which all tend to peace." The author declares, "What great progress!" The essay ends saying, "Yes, the era of revolution is drawing to a close; the era of improvements is beginning. The improvement of nations leaves the violent form and takes a peaceful form; the time is come when Providence will substitute for the disorderly action of agitators, the religious and calm action of peacemakers."[53] No wonder Campbell enthusiastically commended the paper; his own optimistic vision of peace and progress are so well represented in its words.

At the end of his life Campbell's confidence was severely shaken by the cataclysm of civil war forcing him to attach his hope to something other than divinely directed progress. He kept his eyes looking forward toward the Peaceable Kingdom though he was forced to admit that the course of its arrival would not be as he had anticipated. Still, his commitment to nonviolence was firm to the end. He saw it as a practice suitable for a people seeking to follow Christ and endeavoring to live in light of the coming Millennium. This will be discussed further in the following two chapters.

## Notes

1. *Millennial Harbinger*, (1848), 371.
2. ibid., 368.
3. ibid., 369.
4. ibid., 369 - 370.
5. ibid., 370.
6. ibid., 374.
7. *The Christian Baptist*, (1825), 283.
8. *Millennial Harbinger*, (1848), 367.
9. ibid., 365.

10. ibid., 367.
11. ibid., 360f.
12. *The Evidences of Christianity: A Debate*, 408ff.
13. *Millennial Harbinger*, (1848), 367.
14. ibid., 373.
15. Cited in Edmond Tabor Linenthal, *Changing Images of the Warrior Hero In America* (New York: Edwin Mellen Press, 1982), 71.
16. *Millennial Harbinger*, (1861), 338.
17. *Millennial Harbinger*, (1848), 373.
18. ibid., 339.
19. ibid., 338.
20. ibid., (1848), 371.
21. ibid., 376.
22. ibid.
23. ibid., 377.
24. *Millennial Harbinger*, (1861), 316.
25. ibid., 338.
26. For example, *Millennial Harbinger*, (1846), 640, 641; (1848), 355, 367; (1861), 339; *The Christian System*, 135.
27. *Millennial Harbinger*, (1861), 338f.
28. ibid., (1846), 640.
29. ibid., 641.
30. ibid.
31. ibid., 354.
32. ibid., (1848), 375.
33. ibid.
34. S. Morris Eames, *The Philosophy of Alexander Campbell* (Bethany, W. Va.: Bethany College, 1966), 75.
35. *Millennial Harbinger*, (1848), 384.
36. ibid., (1850), 523.
37. ibid., 524.
38. ibid., (1848), 364.
39. ibid.
40. ibid., 363.
41. ibid., 379.
42. ibid., 380.
43. ibid.
44. ibid., 381.

45. ibid.
46. ibid., (1850), 523.
47. ibid., (1834), 482.
48. ibid., 483.
49. ibid.
50. ibid., 549.
51. ibid., (1835), 105.
52. ibid., 703.
53. ibid., 706.

## Chapter 3

# Campbell's Eschatology and His Pacifist Ethics

Pacifism is not an ethical oddity unconnected with the main themes of Alexander Campbell's thought. Rather pacifism is intimately connected with the abiding concerns that occupied his theological work through the years. This is certainly true in relation to Campbell's view of the kingdom of God. "In the systematizing of Mr. Campbell's doctrinal ideas," wrote W.E. Garrison, "the central place must be given to his idea of the Kingdom of God."[1]

Of course, it was not in Campbell's thinking alone that the kingdom of God played an important role. A lively anticipation of the divine kingdom permeated much of nineteenth century American religious thought. Francis Wayland, president of Brown University and leading philosopher, much admired by Campbell, spoke for many in saying, "Perhaps before the youth of this generation have been gathered to their fathers, there may burst forth upon these highly-favored States the light of Millennial Glory. What is to prevent it? I do believe that the option is put into our hands... The church has for two thousand years been praying, 'Thy kingdom come.' Jesus is saying unto us, 'It shall come if you desire it.'"[2] The conviction that the kingdom of God could be ushered in by human effort spurred reformers to work diligently to rid society of a variety of injustices and sins. This was certainly the case for peace reformers who believed nonviolence was essential for the kingdom to come.

While peace activists and pacifists of every stripe worked in hope of the millennium, they did not all share the same vision and methods. Still, they all agreed that Christ's reign on earth could not be instituted by force. The renunciation of war and the adoption of a life of nonviolent love were seen as essential, but beyond this consensus there was little unity. Those among the American Peace Society, the largest peace organization in the nineteenth century United

States, believed the path to the millennium came by way of education and the reform of existing institutions. War could be abolished if nations were taught alternative ways of resolving disputes. They advocated the formation of a World Congress that would mediate conflicts and facilitate understanding and cooperation between nations.

Left wing peace activists were suspicious of nation-centered efforts. The radical pacifists, or non-resistants, such as William Lloyd Garrison and Henry Clark Wright, believed the social and political institutions were beyond redemption. They called upon men and women to renounce all violence and separate themselves from the corrupt organizations of the world. As Valarie Ziegler put it, "The sectarian non-resistants wanted to turn the world upside down, whereas the cultural Christians of the American Peace Society were content to fine tune it."[3] Still both groups believed that the kingdom would come if they could persuade others to follow the Prince of Peace. Campbell shared their hope, but he looked to the restored church rather than a morally improved society as the key to open the door to the millennium.

## Forms of the Kingdom

Campbell believed that the kingdom of God always existed, but was not always in one and the same form. He held that as with earthly kingdoms, so too with God's kingdom, five essential elements must be present: king, constitution, subjects, laws, and territory.[4] While these five elements were always present, they were so in three distinct forms, corresponding to the three dispensations he identified in his biblical hermeneutics already briefly described in the first chapter.

The first of these dispensations Campbell called the "Patriarchal age of the world."[5] It was a time of the family-worship institution. There were family altars, but not public altars, temples, well-developed order of priests or other large institutions. At the center of this dispensation were two promises made to Abraham: "I will make of you a great nation," and "In your seed shall all nations of the earth be blessed." These two promises point toward the two dispensations, which were to come.[6]

The first promise was a promise of land for the chosen nation, Israel. The second promise was the promise of Christ who would bless the entire world through his kingdom, the church. The Patriarchal age lasted from Adam to the time of Moses. During this period God progressively revealed such matters as the Sabbath law, the practice of circumcision, the distinction between clean and unclean objects and animals, and the idea of animal sacrifice. The Patriarchal age was preparatory for the next expression of the kingdom of God, which was found in the Jewish dispensation.

In the Jewish dispensation God's kingdom was embodied in a national form. Campbell marked the beginning of the second dispensation with the giving of the Ten Commandments on Mt. Sinai.[7] God promised to be the Hebrew people's God and to bless the nation with prosperity, protection, health and national success if they were faithfully obedient. The standards and ordinances of the first dispensation were in effect in the second dispensation only to the extent that God explicitly reinstated them. During this second dispensation national political life, the priesthood, the festivals, the tabernacle and then the temple, and the highly developed system of laws and rituals were instituted by the revelation of God. Campbell believed that the particulars of the rule of God during the Jewish dispensation were preparatory for the final Christian dispensation.

W.E. Garrison observed that "the Jewish dispensation was not intended so much to effect the eternal salvation of those under it, as to preserve the knowledge of God, to exhibit His virtues and to show the advantages of service to Him."[8] But for Campbell this did not lessen the importance of the Jewish dispensation. He held that it was not possible for anyone to genuinely understand the kingdom of God present in the Christian dispensation who had not studied the dialect of the antecedent administrations of heaven over the patriarchs and Jews.[9]

With each succeeding dispensation, the kingdom of God broadened in scope, from family, to nation, to world. Campbell referred to the kingdom of God in the Christian dispensation as "the kingdom of heaven" because it is not a kingdom of this world.[10] Yet the kingdom has a presence in the world in the form of churches, or what Campbell called "congregations of the Lord."[11] He held that this third dispensation began on the first Pentecost after the ascension of Christ to the right hand of God. It was then, Campbell believed, that God gave the kingdom to Christ to rule.[12] Unlike the detailed system of laws that guided the Jews, the law of love – love for God and love for other people – was the spring from which flowed every other Christian obligation.

Campbell saw no evangelistic mandate in earlier expressions of the kingdom of God. However, the kingdom of heaven, the church, was "to enlighten and convert the world."[13] Campbell used military imagery in describing the work of the church. He spoke of Christians as soldiers at war against unrighteousness and falsehood. This imagery in no way condoned literal warfare but graphically indicated the necessity of discipline, training and sacrifice as Christians carry out the mission God had given the church. He was careful to point out that Christians "have not to wrestle with flesh and blood, but with the rulers of the darkness of this world – with spiritual wickedness in high places,"[14] referring as he had on other occasions to Paul's words in the sixth chapter of Ephesians.

Though Campbell called the church the kingdom of heaven and the kingdom of God, he conceded that the two "do not always or exactly represent the same thing."[15] Members of the church are the citizens of the kingdom of God, but the kingdom of God would finally be displayed in "the universal subjugation of the nations to the scepter of Jesus" which, Campbell believed, would come about when there was "a general restoration of all the institutions of the Kingdom of Heaven in their primitive character."[16] In other words, as the church acted to restore primitive Christianity, the way would open for the universal triumph of God over the corrupt powers of the world bringing about the millennium, the reign of utopian bliss on earth prior to the return of Christ.

## The Millennium

Millennial hope flourished in nineteenth century America. To a great extent these hopes were pinned on an optimistic assessment of the prospects of the nation. Many of the leading voices in religion held that the fortunes of God's kingdom and the fortunes of America were largely one and the same.[17] H. Richard Niebuhr observed, "As the Nineteenth century went on, the note of divine favoritism were increasingly sounded. Christianity, democracy, Americanism, the English language and culture, the growth of industry and science, American institutions – these are all confounded and confused."[18] While Alexander Campbell shared the prevalent millennial hope, he did not – at least in his earlier years – understand the millennium as contingent upon or identical to the success of America. Rather, "only the restored church, he thought, could produce the unity in both church and society that was requisite to the millennial age."[19]

Campbell held that preparation for the millennial age required the restoration of the church according to the ancient order as presented in the New Testament. Early in his ministry Campbell wrote that "just in so far as the ancient order of things, or the religion of the New Testament, is restored, just so far has the Millennium commenced."[20] The recovery of the pure and innocent past was intimately connected with the inception of the perfect future. As Campbell envisioned this age of peace and plenty called the millennium, it was incompatible with the disharmony of disputing denominations. Peace had to be practiced in the church before the reign of peace could ensue throughout the world.

Campbell believed peaceful unity among Christians and churches would occur only as human creeds and traditions were set aside in favor of the ancient gospel. He wrote,

> All religious denominations are shaking... But of all the means which can be employed to promote peace on earth and good will among men, which have any influence to destroy sectarianism, or which are at all adapted to introduce the millennium [sic] there is none to compare with the simple proclamation of the ancient gospel.[21]

In introducing his new periodical *Millennial Harbinger* Campbell stated that the aim of the journal was to accomplish "the destruction of Sectarianism, Infidelity, and Anti-christian doctrine and practice." Further, he stated that the new journal would seek to foster "the development, and introduction of that political and religious order of society called THE MILLENNIUM, which will be the consummation of that ultimate amelioration of society proposed in the Christian Scriptures."[22]

This "ancient order" Campbell advocated required the repudiation as tests of fellowship all divisive elements of belief and theological speculations which are not explicitly a part of the essential biblical faith. The beliefs that distinguish one denomination from another cannot, according to Campbell, foster unity or promote the millennium. "We assume it for a principle, that the union of Christians, and the destruction of sects, are indispensable prerequisites to the subjection of the world to the government of Jesus, and to the triumphant appearance of Christ's religion in the world."[23]

His early biographer and friend Robert Richardson stated that Campbell believed there were no other viable means of preparing the world for the reign of Christ than the one Campbell himself proposed. "He felt assured that a reformation such as he advocated, which proposed to go back to the very beginning and restore the gospel in its original purity and fullness, could leave no room for any other religious reformation, and must of necessity, be the very last effort possible to prepare the world for the coming Christ."[24] The restoration of the "ancient order" was not merely a conservative retreat to an idyllic past. Rather, for Campbell the restoration was an indispensable means to a divinely promised future. Campbell believed that if God's design for the church was regained, this would open the way for Christ's reign on earth in the not so distant future.[25]

Campbell had no interest in predicting dates or describing specific prophesied "signs of the times" associated with the inception of the millennium.[26] He did not anticipate a cataclysmic end of the world brought about by the return of Christ, as did his pre-millennialist contemporary, William Miller. Rather Campbell was a postmillennialist who held that the influence of the gospel would spread to such an extent that a millennial reign of peace and prosperity would occur, after which Christ would return in glory. In 1841 he wrote on the "Protestant Theory" of the coming of the Lord, stating:

> The Millennium... will be a state of greatly enlarged and continuous prosperity, in which the Lord will be exalted and his divine spirit enjoyed in an unprecedented measure. All the conditions of society will be vastly improved; wars shall cease, and peace and good will among men will generally abound... Genuine Christianity will be diffused through all nations; crimes and punishments will cease; governments will recognize human rights, and will rest on just and benevolent principles.[27]

He went on to speak of how even the seasons and climates will become more mild and pleasant, health for all will improve, work will become less burdensome, soil more fertile, and animal life more abundant.[28]

One year earlier, in his debate with Robert Owen, Campbell proclaimed his confident hope for a state of society like nothing yet experienced on earth:

> Fancy to yourselves, my friends, a society in which such [good and faithful] characters shall have the rule, and then you want no poet to describe the millennium to you. Peace, harmony, love, and universal goodness, must be the order of the day. There wants nothing - believe me, my friends, there wants nothing - but the restoration of ancient Christianity, and a cordial reception of it, to fill the world with all the happiness, physical, intellectual, and moral, which beings like us in the state of trial could endure - shall I say? - yes, endure, and enjoy.[29]

## Eschatology and Action

David Edwin Harrell, Jr. has observed, "The social implications of post-millennialism are both obvious and profound. Optimism, a belief in progress, and a desire for reform are inherent in such a religious interpretation of history."[30] People tend to prepare for the future they anticipate and in their preparations they help bring about that future. This was certainly true for Alexander Campbell and other reformers. In addition to his determination to overcome division within the church and to free the scriptures from creedal encumberments, he listed other socially significant aims for his journal, the *Millennial Harbinger*. These include addressing the "inadequacy of all the present systems of education, literary and oral, to develop the powers of the human mind, and to prepare man for rational and social happiness."[31]

Campbell also declared his intention to call into question American laws and policies that fell short of biblical standards and eschatological visions of justice. He was determined to speak to the "injustice which yet remains in many of the political regulations under the best political governments, when contrasted with the justice which Christianity proposes, and which the millennial order of society promises."[32] Further, Campbell placed on his agenda, "Disquisitions upon the treatment of African slaves, as preparatory to their emancipation and exaltation from their present degraded condition."[33] Thus he announced he had no intention of passively waiting for the millennium. Rather his desire was to promote in the present actions that were a reflection of the future reign of Christ, which he believed was drawing near.

Many who eagerly anticipated the millennium failed to see the relationship of pacifism to that age of divine blessing. Writing in 1836 in his very popular *The Manual of Peace* Thomas Upham, professor of moral philosophy in Bowdoin College, declared that one view of the subject of peace that "almost entirely escaped notice was this: War in all its forms is obviously inconsistent with the millennial state."[34] He went on to say that the principles that will guide life in the millennium are to be practiced in the present. All contention and disunity will end and the hearts of people everywhere will be bound together by the power of the gospel if people will obey Christ.

There is, according to Upham, no justification for waiting until a later time before adopting a mode of life suitable for God's kingdom. There is not one set of moral standards prior to the millennium and a different set of standards to be put in effect after the beginning of the millennium. Upham maintained "if it will not be right to take life and carry on war in the millennium, it is not right to take life and carry on war now." He emphasized, "The very principles, which will be acknowledged as authoritative in the millennium, are the very principles which are prescribed and are binding upon us at the present moment."[35] While this point may have "almost entirely escaped the notice" of many, as Upham claimed, it certainly was not lost on Alexander Campbell. In this matter, Campbell and Upham thought very much alike.

Campbell recognized nonviolence as among the behaviors necessary for those who were preparing for the coming reign of Christ. "The fullness of time is come. Messiah appears," he wrote.[36] Contrasting the victories of military leaders with their armies who came devastating nations and humiliating their enemies, Campbell spoke of the triumph of Christ as being "the conquest of all temptations, of death, and of him that had the power of death."[37] As Campbell envisioned it, the victory of Christ over evil was not wrought by brute force and physical violence, but by spiritual power and truth exhibited in the lives of Christ's followers. The light of the coming reign of Christ, he believed, should impel disciples to repudiate war and the passions from which war arises. Campbell wrote,

> The precepts of his institution correspond with his appearance and deportment among men. He inculcates a morality pure as himself, and such as must render his disciples superior to all the world besides. He gives no

> scope to any malignant passions, and checks every principle that would lead to war, oppression, or cruelty. His precepts respect not merely the overt act, but the principles from which all overt acts of wickedness proceed.[38]

But even before Christ's universal reign of peace, "the principles of his government" are active in the lives of his subjects "to give them a taste of, and a taste for, heavenly things."[39] Campbell believed that for Christians the future is already present, not in its entirety but in anticipatory ways, forming a people suitable for the millennial age.

In "An Oration in Honor of the Fourth of July, 1830", Campbell sketched his understanding of the history of the world leading up to "the Reign of Heaven" when Christ comes to establish a government of a new order. Ultimately, Christ will "subvert all political government, the very best as well as the very worst..." and he will then "govern the world by religion only." The earthly powers will "literally 'beat their swords into ploughshares and their spears into pruning-hooks, and learn war no more.'"[40]

The ethically formative power of the God-promised future was discussed by Campbell in his debate with Robert Owen. Campbell distinguished two possible ways eschatology could be related to ethics. With the first, threats of punishment and promises of reward serve as a basis for compelling desirable behavior. In the second, people are presented with a vision of the good and perfect future intended by God and they are thereby inspired to live in the present in a manner that will prepare them to enjoy the perfection to come. The first approach is characterized by censure and restrictive laws. The second, according to Campbell, "aims not at reforming or happifying the world by a system of legal restraints, however excellent, but its immediate object is to implant in the human heart, through the discovery of divine philanthropy, a principle of love, which fulfills every moral precept ever promulgated on earth." Stressing the peace-inspiring power of Christianity, Campbell declared, "Here is the grand secret: the religion of Jesus Christ melts the hearts of men into pure philanthropy. It converts a lion into a lamb."[41]

Legalistic means of controlling behavior, Campbell contended, leads to little happiness. Law is not capable of producing happiness since law restrains rather than liberates and "to restrain a person is to diminish his enjoyment." Consequently, "the only happiness good men derive from law is protection."[42]

Campbell held that the reason why the world is not a much more happy place is because people have corrupted Christianity by codifying it into a rigid system of laws and ceremonies. Under the reign of Christ, peace-making love is the dominant principle. "The genius of Christianity is love," wrote Campbell. "Its tendency is peace on earth and good-will among men-and it will eventuate in glory to God and man in the highest heaven. It contemplates the reformation of the world upon a new principle. It aims at conquering men by love."[43]

Laws for the present and threats of future punishment can never touch the deepest levels of human nature. Actions may be altered but hidden intentions remain the same. Only superficial changes are made by laws, claimed Campbell. "Letters only reach the eyes, but favor can touch the heart. Laws expressed in words assail the ears and aim at restraining actions; but love pierces to the heart, and disarms the rising thought of mischievous intent."[44] Laws and the threat of punishment keep people in bondage. They have no power to elevate people as children of God, suitable for the kingdom of heaven.

Campbell recognized that governing authorities at times sought to manipulate Christian eschatological beliefs for their own ends. In his debate with Owen, Campbell quoted with approval a passage from English pacifist Soame Jenyns on this issue. Jenyns maintained that authorities had sometimes employed the belief in a future life of rewards and punishments in order to sanction laws and motivate the sort of behavior desirable for an orderly society. The goodness sought, however, was not in order to serve God's purpose but to be useful in meeting the needs of the state. This approach may "help develop good citizens: but is not likely to produce genuine Christians."[45] True Christian ethics, Campbell recognized, was neither defined by social utility nor motivated by fear of the future.

Campbell taught that the ethical standards of the future realm are in effect in the present time. Already in the present the reign of Christ has power "to render us fit members of a celestial society hereafter."[46] Only an ethics rooted in heaven could bring about a transformation of heart, mind and life which reflects the reality of heaven, believed Campbell. The role of law might help remedy a corrupt present but Christ's rule of love heralds a perfect future. Campbell wrote of Christ's reign, "It is called the reign of Heaven, because down into the heart it draws the heavenly feelings, desires and aim. From heaven it came, and to heaven it leads. "I will shake the heavens and the earth," says the Lord. "I will revolutionize the world; and how, my friends, but by introducing new principles of human action?"[47] Christ made clear that these new principles are guided by a love that leaves no room for any old "principle that would lead to war, oppression or cruelty."[48]

The meaning of Christian ethics for Campbell could not be exhausted in any this-worldly usefulness. Christians were not simply to cope effectively with the problems of the present but to ready themselves for the divine realm yet to come. Campbell wrote, "That the tendency of this religion is to produce purity of heart as essential to present and future happiness; not to obtain it as a reward, but to prepare ourselves for the enjoyment of it."[49] Christian life could not at any time be determined by the hostilities of the present but must always be lived in view of the coming reign of peace.

Campbell depicted Christ as a conqueror at war, intent on increasing his realm. But this war that he wages with the support of his subjects is unlike any earthly conflict because the "cardinal principle in his government is love." Campbell continued,

> He subdues by no other sword than that of the Spirit. Other kings subdue men's persons and hold a sovereignty over their enemies, but he seizes the hearts of men. To conquer enemies is his grand enterprise. Philosophy as well as religion teaches us that to conquer enemies is not the work of swords, or lances, or bows of steel. It is not to bind men's persons to a triumphal car, to incarcerate them in strong holds, or to make them surrender to superior bravery, prowess and strength. To conquer an enemy is to convert him into a friend. This is the noble, benevolent and heaven-conceived enterprise of God's only-begotten Son. To do this all arms and modes of warfare are impotent, save the arms and munitions of everlasting love. By vivid displays of God's philanthropy he approaches his enemies, and by the arguments with which this eloquence is fraught he addresses a rebel world. Such is his mode of warfare; a system devised in heaven, and like all of God's means, perfectly adapted to the high ends proposed.[50]

Campbell reminded his listeners that "this world is to be revolutionized" by followers of Christ through the use of no other weapon than the "true gospel" which is "the sword of the Eternal Spirit."[51] He was convinced that only nonviolent love, guided by the gospel was "God's means, perfectly adapted to the high ends proposed," those ends being social transformation in light of the coming universal reign of Christ. Worldly weapons were impotent to accomplish such an end. Only the gospel of God's love was adequate. "By it alone," wrote Campbell, "proclaimed and proved and sustained in the lives of its advocates, were the Jewish and Pagan institutions of former ages supplanted by the Christians, and that great change in society affected which is still blessing the earth with peace and goodwill."[52]

Similar themes are present in Campbell's writings nearly two decades later. In summing up the points he made in his "An Address on War," Campbell again called attention to the eschatological dimension of his pacifism. "The prophecies clearly indicate that the Messiah himself would be 'the Prince of Peace,' and that under his reign 'wars should cease,' and 'nations study it no more.'"[53] But while wars had not yet ceased, Campbell held that the future of Christ's peaceful reign over the world must be prefigured or foreshadowed in the present by the people who had by faith seen the future in Christ, and had begun living peaceful and loving lives. Passive waiting was unacceptable to him. And so Campbell concluded, "Let everyone, then, who fears God and loves man, put his hand to the work; and the time is not far distant, when:

'No longer hosts encountering hosts
Shall crowds of slain deplore;
They'll hang the trumpet in the hall
And study war no more!'[54]

## Notes

1. Winfred Ernest Garrison, *Alexander Campbell's Theology: Its Sources and Historical Setting* (St. Louis: Christian Publishing Company, 1900), 161.
2. Francis Wayland, "Encouragements to Religious Efforts," in *American National Preacher*, Vol. 5, No. 3 (1830), 39-46, cited in James F. Maclear, "The Republic and the Millennium," in John M. Mulder and John F. Wilson, ed. *Religion in American History: Interpretive Essays* (Englewood Cliff, N.J.: Prentice-Hall, 1978), 188-189.
3. Valarie H. Ziegler, *The Advocates of Peace in Antebellum America* (Bloomington: Indiana University Press, 1992), 15.

4. Alexander Campbell, *The Christian System* (Nashville: Gospel Advocate, 1964), 125.
5. ibid., 108.
6. ibid., 113.
7. ibid., 121.
8. Garrison, op. cit., 173f.
9. *The Christian System*, 119.
10. ibid., 127.
11. ibid., 133.
12. ibid., 137ff.
13. ibid., 134.
14. ibid., 135.
15. ibid., 147.
16. ibid., 153.
17. see J.F. Maclear, "The Republic and the Millennium," *The Religion of the Republic*, Elwyn A. Smith, ed. (Philadelphia: Fortress Press, 1971), 183-216.
18. H. Richard Niebuhr, *The Kingdom of God in America* (New York: Harper & Row, 1937), 179.
19. Richard T. Hughes, "From Primitive Church to Civil Religion: the Millennial Odyssey of Alexander Campbell," *Journal of the American Academy of Religion*, 88.
20. *The Christian Baptist*, 1825, 136.
21. ibid., 1827, 251ff.
22. *Millennial Harbinger*, 1830, 1f.
23. ibid., 55.
24. Robert Richardson, *Memoirs of Alexander Campbell*, II (Philadelphia: J.B. Lippencott & Co., 1896), 302f.
25. Robert T. Hughes, "The Apocalyptic Origins of the Churches of Christ and the Triumph of Modernism," *Religion and American Culture*, 2, 2 (Summer, 1992).
26. Winfred Ernest Garrison and Alfred T. DeGroot, *The Disciples of Christ: A History* (St. Louis: Christian Board of Publication, 1948), 206.
27. *Millennial Harbinger*, 1841, 9.
28. ibid.
29. Alexander Campbell and Robert Owen, *The Evidences of Christianity: A Debate* (St. Louis: Christian Board of Publication, n.d.), 395.
30. David Edwin Harrell, Jr., *Quest for a Christian American: The Disciples of Christ and American Society to 1866* (Nashville: The Disciples of Christ Historical Society, 1966), 40.
31. *Millennial Harbinger*, 1830, 1.
32. ibid.
33. ibid.
34. Thomas C. Upham, *The Manual of Peace* (New York: Leavill, Lord & Co., 1836, 141.
35. ibid., 144.

36. *The Christian Baptist*, 1823, 13.
37. ibid.
38. ibid.
39. Alexander Campbell, *Popular Lectures and Addresses* (Philadelphia: James Challen & Son, 1864), 371.
40. ibid., 374.
41. Alexander Campbell and Robert Owen, *The Evidences of Christianity: A Debate*, 396.
42. ibid., 395.
43. ibid., 403.
44. ibid., 397.
45. ibid., 405.
46. ibid.
47. ibid., 397.
48. *Christian Baptist*, 1823, 12.
49. *Evidences of Christianity*, 406.
50. ibid.
51. ibid., 377.
52. ibid.
53. ibid., 362.
54. ibid., 366.

## Chapter 4

# Millennial America and The Vision of Peace

Up until the mid-1840's, Alexander Campbell had little to say about America's role in relation to the millennium – that perfectly harmonious, just and joyful reign of the Lord prophesied in scripture. However, this silence lifted during his later years. The first indication of this change was seen in 1841; in an address entitled "On Common Schools" Campbell stressed the importance of public education for the good of the entire community. He argued however that a dissemination of information was not sufficient; moral education was imperative and the Bible must be central to any moral education. He claimed that clergy of all denominations agreed with him. Campbell continued:

> It is also becoming more and more evident that, notwithstanding our sectarian differences, we yet have something called a common Christianity; – that there are certain great fundamental matters – indeed, every thing elementary in what is properly called piety and morality – in which all good men of all denominations are agreed; and that these great common principles and views form a common ground on which all Christian people can unite, harmonize and co-operate in one great system of moral and Christian education.[1]

Thirteen years later Campbell went further still and claimed that the United States had "a by law established religion." This religion was not denominational, he asserted, and did not have a specific form of worship. Nevertheless, it was evident in the administration of oaths, the conscience of the population and appeals to God made at every level of the government. "In these we have a solemn recognition of the being and perfection of God, of a day of judgment, or future and eternal rewards and punishments."[2] This common religion, Campbell recognized, was a nonsectarian Protestantism.

## The Role of America

While Campbell never repudiated his belief in the centrality of the restored church in preparing the world for the millennium, the United States came to have an increasingly larger role in his thinking. In fact, Ernest Lee Tuveson wrote of Campbell, "No other preacher more completely fused the religious and secular elements of the millennial utopia; none more strongly emphasized the need for social reform as preparation for the great age."[3] Campbell held that the American situation was ideal because it "conforms to the genius of human nature and human society, as developed in the Christian Scriptures."[4]

Campbell refused to acknowledge that the Deist views of the founders of the nation played a significant role shaping any characteristic of American life that could help inaugurate the millennium.[5] "We are indebted for all the great improvements in society for the philosophy of Christians," declared Campbell, "and not to the philosophy of skeptics ... The labors of the Reformers, and the more recent labors of Milton, the poet, and Locke, the philosopher, have done more to create the free institutions of Europe and America than the labors of all the skeptics."[6] There was no intrinsic quality that set America apart from other nations. The greatness Campbell found in the United States – and in England – was not a matter of climate, geography or race but rather could be attributed to the influence of the Bible and Protestantism.[7] Campbell began to teach that the liberation of the world from spiritual darkness and oppression was the destiny of "Protestant America and Protestant England."[8] The destiny of Protestantism is bound up in the country's destiny and in Protestantism's destiny that of all the nations of the world. "God has given, in awful charge, to Protestant England and Protestant America – the Anglo-Saxon race – the fortunes, not of Christendom only, but of all the world."[9]

In earlier years, Campbell held that there was no "common religion" that might lead to the unity of the church, and through the church, to the unity and peace of the world, except in the restored gospel that he proclaimed. Richard T. Hughes suggested that the results of Campbell's restoration movement were not up to his expectations. Consequently, he shifted his millennial hopes from the church to the nation that he saw successfully embodying the unity in diversity he hoped to achieve in the church.[10]

It came to be Campbell's conviction that America would be able to drive out ignorance, superstition and injustice by being an example of freedom, education, progress and faith. All that needed to be done in order to benefit the nations and peoples of the world would be for Americans to "show them our religion by pointing to our common schools, our common churches, our common colleges and our common respect for the Bible, the Christian religion and its divine and glorious Founder – the Supreme Philanthropist"[11] Campbell was confident that the influence of Britain and the United States would continue to spread to every nation throughout the world. He looked forward with assurance to the day when the nations "Hang their trumpet in the hall, and study war no more. Peace and universal amity will reign triumphant. For over all the earth there will be but one Lord, one faith, one hope and one language" – English![12]

## America in the Peace Movement

Campbell certainly was not the only antebellum pacifist who believed America was to have a central role in the inauguration of the millennium. One of the more interesting developments in the arguments against war was the emphasis placed on "the special mission of the United States" as a vanguard for peace.[13] Speaking before the Hartford Peace Society, the Rev. N.S. Wheaton said, "The free and enlightened citizens of America have given proof that they are breaking through the trammels of an accursed delusion [of war], under which the world has lain spellbound for ages."[14] Not only had monarchist tyranny and oppressive superstition been dealt a blow by freedom-filled America, but God was also using America to lead the world to turn from the ways of war.

American Peace Society President, William Ladd, repeatedly claimed that the United States had a distinctive responsibility to cast war as a benighted practice of the Old World in order to lead the nations to harmony and peace. Likewise, Samuel E. Coves, Ladd's immediate successor as president of the Society wrote, "It is in this country that the martial spirit has received its greatest check. It is here that the pacific principles will first be adopted."[15] Coves argued that war was contrary to the democratic spirit that was the lifeblood of America. The practice of war, he believed, could not long endure in a nation populated by citizens with equal rights.

This opinion was shared by Elihur Burritt, a brilliant and largely self-taught energetic peace activist who was sometimes referred to as the "learned blacksmith." Burritt founded the League of Universal Brotherhood in 1846 after conservatives took control of the American Peace Society. He wrote in the pages of his journal on New Year's Day 1845: "I find my mind is setting with all its sympathies toward the subject of Peace. I am persuaded that it is reserved to crown the destiny of America, that she shall be the great peacemaker in the brotherhood of nations."[16]

Pacifists in other countries occasionally asserted that their particular nations were destined to usher in worldwide peace. But such claims were much more common from advocates of peace in America. Nowhere else did millennial hopes run so high.

## Nonviolent Americanism

Like other nineteenth century pacifists, Campbell saw no contradiction between his millennial hope in America and his commitment to peace. In fact it was to the pacifist leader Thomas Grimké that Campbell is indebted for the idea that Anglo-Saxon superiority arises from Protestantism.[17] He imagined a world eager to be Americanized and by being Americanized, Christianized. Resistance to the destiny of America was virtually unthinkable. Campbell seemed unwilling to entertain the possibility that the United States, God's instrument for liberation, might be required to use deadly force to achieve the noble ends he envisioned. In his optimism, he failed to recognize that "America's national origin, and the first expressions of national character were largely military in form."[18] Only with a self-imposed amnesia could Campbell forget that the expansion of the nation had already displaced and killed hundreds of thousands of Native Americans and Mexicans.

Campbell apparently was convinced that the power of reason, persuasion, and truth would nonviolently overcome any pockets of resistance to the mission of America. He even called upon his readers, not just to cherish "but prosecute, the duties which we owe to ourselves, our country and the human race." For only in so doing, "will our career be glorious, our end victorious, and our destiny, and that of our country, 'fair as the moon, clear as the sun,' and to our enemies 'terrible as an army with banners.'"[19]

Still Campbell would never condone any literal "army with banners." Despite the bloated claims that he sometimes made regarding the destiny of American, his pacifism tempered his views. As much as Campbell exalted America and gloried in its millennial role, he recognized that the nation's civilization would not be sufficiently developed until there would be no room for selfishness, hatred, revenge, terror and cruelty. Civilization cannot be complete until society reaches "that intellectual, benevolent, pacific, moral and blissful goal."[20] He never advocated holy wars of liberation as a possible means of spreading the good he believed America had to offer to the world. For Campbell such holy wars would be fratricide. In his essay "The Destiny of our Country," he reminded his audience, "Nations and empires stand to each other as members of an individual family stand to one another."[21]

The universalism of Campbell's pacifism helped to thwart any tendency to promote the national good at the expense of other nations and peoples. In an essay in which he asserted that the civilizations of Europe and America have a "present superiority over their more remote ancestors, and over all other portions of the human race,"[22] he made no attempt to use this claim to justify the subjugation of others. Rather, Campbell insisted that "the amelioration of the social state" could never be in reference only "to that little community of which we may happen to be a component part; but to that great community of communities which fills up the whole circle of our national intercourse" and which grows "from nation to nation."[23]

Amazingly, even after making the most extravagant claims for the millennial role of America, Campbell would check himself. Citing the pacifist Soame Jenyns, Campbell stated, "Patriotism, it is conceded, has no special place in the Christian religion. Its founder never pronounced a single sentence in commendation of it." As Campbell knew, Jesus Christ had a love that recognized no borders, "and as patriotism is only an extension of the principle of selfishness," patriotism being a love of what is one's own, "he deigned it no regard, because selfishness is the great damning sin of mankind."[24]

A quarter century earlier, in his debate with Robert Owens, Campbell approvingly referred to Jenyns' claim that patriotism is a pagan virtue. Campbell never backed away from that view. He conceded that "our neighbor is every man in the world," but inasmuch as no one can directly love everyone in the world, Campbell argued, "Our country, then, for the most part engages our attention, and exhausts all our means of doing good." Consequently, by increasing the morality, prosperity and character of the nation, Christians "extend its means of communicating blessing which, without it, no Christian man could bestow upon his species."[25]

This approach sounds like a "trickle-down" blessedness. However, it is not significantly different from his teachings about patriotism prior to the development of his understanding of the millennial role of America. In 1832, he distinguished "Christian philanthropy" from the "love of country" exhibited by the patriot. Campbell's objection to patriotism implied nothing critical of the natural affection for one's own country. Rather he opposed that patriotism which promotes the love for and promotion of the interests of one's country at the expense of other peoples and nations or to the neglect of the needs of those beyond the boundaries of one's own country.[26] For Campbell, the universality of Christian love must always challenge the parochial impulses of patriotism.

## Peaceful Reign Delayed

A few years prior to the beginning of the Civil War, Campbell began to express doubts about an imminent beginning of the millennium and he fell silent about any millennial role for America. In 1858, Campbell mentioned hearing from a Washington correspondent who stated that a spiritual awakening had been detected throughout the land. The writer suggested that perhaps this "may be the herald of the millennium." Campbell did not agree. He declared that other events, which had not yet occurred, must precede the millennium. Among these, he wrote, "The sword is to be beat into the pruning hook, the lion and the lamb lie down together, and the nations of the earth are to learn war no more." But as Campbell looked across the United States and beyond he found the opposite. Preparations for war were more prominent than efforts toward peace. "The sheen of the sword, the bayonet, and the deep mouthed cannon are preserved among all nations, by the constant threat of invasion from abroad, or eruption within."[27]

Again in 1859, there was indication that Campbell's optimism about an imminent inception of the millennium had diminished. He quoted at length a report on the battle at Castiglione between the French and Austrian armies. The report described the horror of the conflict, the agony of the wounded and the grief of the civilians who remained in the town during the battle. At the conclusion of the report, a disheartened Campbell wrote, "The signs of these times are not indicative of the speedy commencement of that long wished for and prayed for era, when the knowledge of the true and only Potentate – 'the King of kings' and the 'Lord of lords' – shall cover the earth as the waters spread themselves over its lakes and seas and oceans."[28] The hope Campbell once had for a prompt inception of the millennium was greatly diminished by the lack of progress toward peace in both the divided church and the divisive nation.

This new train of thought continued into the next few years. Early in 1861 he wrote that the future destiny of the universe was known to God alone. Referring to the millennial reign, he wrote, "And one day being with the Lord of the universe as a thousand years, and a thousand years being as one day, we may on all our premises anticipate a glorious consummation of the present campaign in some one hundred and forty years hence."[29] Later the same year, shortly after the Civil War began, Campbell pushed the millennium into a more distant future by saying before "the actual reign of the Messiah over all the nations, kindreds, tongues and people, can culminate in all its glory and grandeur, the gospel must be announced to all the nations and peoples on this earth."[30]

When the Civil War began, members of the church Campbell that helped to found traded the "Sword of the Spirit" which is the Word of God for the sword of the battlefield. While some pacifists remained in the ranks of Disciples – particularly in the border states – many others disregarded Campbell's cries for nonviolence and threw themselves into the conflict.[31] David Harrell has written, "As the cries of prophets of peace were slowly overwhelmed by the crescendo of galloping hoofs, clattering caissons, and bellowing demagogues – the sounds of a nation converging on Bull Run – most young Disciples packed their Bibles into saddlebags and rode off to do homage before the altar of Mars."[32]

## Hopes Deferred

For Christians, even the approach of the horrible conflict was a hopeful sign. One writes, commenting on the ever-present sense of "cosmic optimism" in the years immediately prior to the civil war, that there was "a feeling that the millennium, if not at hand, was fast approaching" and that there was a "pervasive millennialism which looked hopefully on the American future as the fulfillment of divine promise."[33] But for all the optimism that was evident in Campbell in earlier years, a dark mood had by this time settled over him. Others may have felt that the war was a stage in America's preparation for a millennial mission. Campbell thought otherwise. He apparently was not convinced that the war was in any way ennobling or purifying. To him, the bloody conflict was not a divinely-willed battle for liberation and righteousness but rebellion against the will of God.

Campbell's hopes of seeing the millennial reign of Christ begin during his lifetime were dashed as national bloodletting began. Neither the restored church that he worked to develop nor what he had called "the most Protestant" of nations he loved brought in the millennium Campbell anticipated.[34] As it became apparent to him that the millennial hope he – at least in part – invested in America was misplaced, he began to speak of the millennium as being far less imminent.

At the outbreak of the Civil War, Campbell lifted his pen to call for peace and to dissuade Christians from participating in the conflict. As he had in the past, Campbell again reminded his readers that "no Christian man who fears God and desires to be loyal to the Messiah, the Prince of Peace, shall be found in the ranks of so unholy a warfare." As he frequently did, Campbell cited Jesus' declaration, "My kingdom is not of this world." He continued, "For the reason that kingdom is established upon the principles of equity, peace and love, it shall endure forever."[35] He knew that the same thing could not be said of America.

It was that kingdom of equity, peace and love that Campbell wanted to promote, rather than ever support or condone killing for kingdoms and governments that depend upon the sword and are destined for demise. Campbell called upon his readers to live in a confident and peaceful manner appropriate for the kingdom of God. "Let the Christian therefore rejoice that his citizenship belongs to a kingdom that cannot be shaken or disturbed."[36]

In 1864, Campbell wrote again of the millennium, but the Republic was given no central role in the divine drama. The church regained the prominence it had in Campbell's earlier eschatological thought, but no longer did he see its triumph near at hand. With a mixture of judgment, heartbreak and hope, he wrote,

> We would rather see only the rosy dawn of a peaceful and triumphant procession of a golden age for the church – to imagine her going forth in her bridal adornments to meet the coming of her Espoused in the garments of joy. But it may not be. Darkness and tempest are round about the habitation of his Throne, and the aspects of the future for the church are

darkly militant... Let us not forget the weapons of our warfare, nor distrust the wisdom and power of our Leader.[37]

# Notes

1. Alexander Campbell, *Popular Lectures and Addresses* (Philadelphia: James Challen & Son, 1864), 259.

2. *Millennial Harbinger*, (1854), 67.

3. Ernest Lee Tuveson, *Redeemer Nation: The Idea of America's Millennial Role* (Chicago: University of Chicago Press, 1968), 217.

4. ibid., 1853, 487.

5. *Popular Lectures and Addresses*, 373.

6. Alexander Campbell and Robert Owen, *The Evidences of Christianity: A Debate* (St. Louis: Christian Board of Publication, n.d.), 395.

7. *Popular Lectures and Addresses*, 373.

8. ibid., 174.

9. ibid., 178.

10. Richard T. Hughes, "From Primitive Church to Protestant Nation: The Millennial Odyssey of Alexander Campbell," *Journal of the American Academy of Religion*, XLIV/1 (March 1976), 96ff.

11. *Popular Lectures and Addresses*, 181.

12. ibid., 44.

13. Curti, *The American Peace Crusade 1815 - 1860* (Durham, NC: Duke University Press, 1929), 53.

14. ibid., 44.

15. ibid.

16. quoted in Peter Brock, *Pacifism in the United States from the Colonial Era to the First World War* (Princeton, NJ: Princeton University Press, 1968), 643.

17. Lunger, *The Political Ethics of Alexander Campbell* (St. Louis: Bethany Press, 1854), 245.

18. Marcus Cunliffe, *Soldiers and Civilians: The Martial Experience in America, 1775-1865* (Boston: Little, Brown and Co., 1968), 68.

19. *Popular Lectures and Addresses*, 179.

20. ibid., 55.

21. ibid., 166.
22. ibid., 49.
23. ibid., 48.
24. ibid., 184.
25. ibid., 185.
26. *The Evidences of Christianity: A Debate*, 409.
27. *Millennial Harbinger*, 1858, 335.
28. ibid., 1859, 519.
29. *Millennial Harbinger*, 1861, 20.
30. ibid., 1861, 426.
31. David Edwin Harrell, Jr., op. cit., 139-173.
32. David Edwin Harrell, Jr., "Disciples of Christ Pacifism in Nineteenth Century Tennessee," *Tennessee Historical Quarterly*, 21/3 (Sept. 1962), 266.
33. George M. Frederickson, *The Inner Civil War* (New York: Harper & Row, 1965), 7.
34. *Millennial Harbinger*, 1853, 488.
35. ibid., 1861, 339.
36. ibid.
37. ibid., 1864, 3f.

# Chapter 5

# Pacifism and Relations with the State

By the very nature of their convictions, pacifists such as Campbell were forced to wrestle with the question of the proper relationship of the Christian to the state. For Anabaptists – at least as they have generally been understood – the question had long since been answered; for them the answer was total withdrawal. But for pacifists who did not share their sectarian perspective, the question was very much alive. And even if they wanted to avoid it, they had opponents that thrust it into their attention.

Dr. William Allen, president of Bowdoin College was among those who would not allow the nineteenth century peace activists to evade the difficulties entailed in their pacifism. He asked: can a person who has rejected as immoral the use of deadly force in international affairs participate in governing a state that continues to employ such force in domestic affairs? Can the domestic work of government be accomplished if all potentially deadly force is renounced? From the perspective of absolute pacifism are Christianity and involvement in government mutually exclusive?[1] Such questions received conflicting answers from antebellum American pacifists.

## Conflicting Alternatives

Tension over the place of government and the role of Christians in it existed from the very beginning of the peace movement. Noah Worcester believed the early church was both nonviolent and positive about the Church's involvement in government. Accordingly, in his efforts toward peace reform, he sought to enlist social institutions, rather than to call Christians to withdraw from them. Among those he persuaded to join with him in forming the Massachusetts Peace Society were William Phillips, the governor of the state, who served as president; Joshua P. Blanshard, a wealthy Boston businessman; Abiel Holmes, father of Oliver Wendell Holmes; and William Ellery Channing, one of the most influential and well-known ministers in the nation. The organization and its members had no interest in overthrowing the present order but sought to Christianize it.[2]

David Low Dodge perceived a greater moral and spiritual distance between the social and political establishment and the will of God than did Worcester and his organization. While the membership of his New York Peace Society contained many eminent citizens, perfectionist ideals were prevalent. Dodge believed the world to be depraved and its institutions far from the kingdom of God. He saw Christians as a redeemed minority at odds with the spirit of the age. Peace was possible, not by human efforts to improve institutions, but only by the spiritual regeneration of sinful people. The state, in Dodge's view, was used by God to maintain some semblance of order in a rebellious world. Coercive and violent methods were sometimes employed by governing authorities to accomplish necessary ends. Christians, however, are to be a peculiar people who live by nonviolent love. The work of the government is contrary to the work of Christians and, therefore, held Dodge, Christians should not participate in government, either by serving as elected officials or even by voting.[3]

This tension continued after the formation of the American Peace Society. For the most part, the leaders of the Society were supportive of the function of government and urged its members to work through political channels. The Society was a self-consciously respectable organization that sought to appeal to the social mainstream. It was anti-war but pro-government. George Ladd saw no conflict between working for peace and participating in the political process. He had the heart and the methods of a moderate. As a close friend and coworker remarked, no one "was more thorough on peace, yet he preached no crusade against church or state, nor allow himself to weaken the foundation of either."[4] The importance he placed upon government is apparent in the fact that throughout his life Ladd tirelessly advocated for the establishment of a congress of nations that would bring together representatives of the various governments around the world to negotiate and resolve conflicts.[5]

Likewise Thomas Grimké never suggested that Christians renounce or retreat from government. A lawyer himself, he never questioned the need for the state. He served in the South Carolina state senate for four years. He took for granted that a Christian could serve as a magistrate. While acknowledging that some coercion may be necessary in order to govern, he rejected the notion that a Christian, whether as an agent of the state or not, has a right to use deadly force. Grimké argued that governing officials should lead the population by adopting nonviolent policies. If the population will not follow, the Christian magistrate should resign.[6]

Another moderate absolute pacifist who recognized the importance of the state and the need for limited coercion in government was Thomas Upham. He maintained that for Christianity "the doctrine is, that human life, both in its individual and corporate state...is INVIOLABLE; that it cannot be taken away from any purpose whatever ... The principles of the gospels are binding upon men in their social capacity." Still Upham argued that the practice of nonviolence does not undermine the work of civil government nor oppose "the exercise of its authority to control and punish" so long as the inviolability of human life is honored. He introduced a concept that he called "noninjurious force." "There are some extreme cases, (very few indeed, but still some extreme cases)" he wrote, "where resistance and the use of force, so far as is necessary to disarm and confine the assailant are justified and a duty."[7]

Members of the New England Non-Resistant Society thought otherwise. Being more in the tradition of Dodge, they believed that the state was beyond redemption. All attempts to reform the state from within were misguided, they held. Civil government persistently usurped the government of God, functioning in a manner contrary to the love taught by Jesus Christ. The constitution of the Non-Resistant Society read, "No one who professes to have the spirit of Christ, can consistently sue a man at law for redress of injuries, or thrust any evil-doer into prison, or fill any office in which he would come under obligation to execute penal enactment or take any part in military service – or acknowledge allegiance to any, human government – or justify any man in fighting in defense of property, liberty, life or religion."[8]

William Lloyd Garrison, a prominent leader in the Non-Resistant Society, was highly critical of those within the American Peace Society who condemned international wars and yet supported the use of violence in dealing with domestic threats. He derisively remarked, "Surely nothing can be more dangerous than the doctrine, that the moral obligations of men change with the latitude and longitude of a place."[9] He saw neither in scriptures nor reason any justification for the notion that an armed force from a foreign country should be met with a nonviolent response, yet from within the nation "not permit any of their number to commit the smallest offense, without subjecting them to pains and penalties."[10]

Garrison's Non-Resistant colleague, the Rev. H.C. Wright, likewise called for the withdrawal from government, by Christians. Even voting was viewed by him as an expression of support for state-sponsored violence. He explained, "All preparations for war, in this nation, are begun at the ballot-box. Voting is the first step... Every ballot contains a threat of death; and he, who casts it, pledges himself to aid the government to execute it. The ballot-box is the first step, the gallows or battlefield the last; and whoever takes the first, must take the last. There is no consistent or honest stopping place between them."[11] The Non-Resistants did not deny the necessity of government in an unconverted world but insisted that Christians have no role in an institution that enforces order by armed might.

In this spectrum of pacifist attitudes toward government, Campbell's place was with themoderates and conservatives. He did not echo the Non-Resistants call to renounce human government as contrary to the government of God. On the other hand, he never urged Christians to immerse themselves in political life. In fact, he was quick to offer words of caution. It is probably fair to say with Roland Bainton that Campbell "accorded somewhat grudging acquiescence" to the state.[12] Still with rare exceptions, he cautiously supported the involvement of Christians in the political process and in the functions of government.

Despite ambiguity and shortcomings, Campbell's view of the place of the Christian and church in relation to the state is still quite clear at points. Campbell believed that government is necessary because of sin and violence in the world. He stated in 1830 that "were men truly religious, political government would be unnecessary."[13] Given the spiritual and moral state of humankind, government is essential to avoid chaos and destruction. Writing in his *The Christian System,* Campbell stated that were it not for the prevalence of injustice and violence "civil government would be wholly unnecessary, and its appendages an excrescence upon society."[14] Still later, he wrote, perhaps in view of those with Non-Resistant commitments, "A wise man will not seek to annihilate any institution that the present constitution of the world, and the conditions of human nature seem to require."[15] In the following year, he stated the matter in stronger terms: "He that argues for the abolition of civil government or for the abolition of statutes given to mankind by God himself ?shocks all common sense."[16]

Campbell believed that government was not merely a product of human necessity but also of divine intention. He spoke of "the government of our own, as well as that of the Lord's, creation and ordination" and repeatedly referred to "the Powers that are ordained by God."[17] Civil government, Campbell declared, is a "divine appendix" which God has added to "the volumes of religion and morality."[18] He went so far as to claim that secular authorities and civil government are "by the grace of God, bestowed upon the world." Without them "neither the church nor the world could exist."[19] The state was listed by Campbell, along with the family and church, as "the three sublimely divine and powerful institutions" which have the "destinies of the world in their hands."[20]

Given the importance that the protection of citizens plays in Campbell's understanding of the state, it is striking that he said so little about how this is to be accomplished. Except when he spoke of capital punishment, he said virtually nothing about the employment of force necessary to preserve life and keep order in a society. This reticence could be due to the optimism he absorbed from Enlightenment influences. Campbell believed that Christians have no role to play in this arena. As Campbell wrote in 1835, "Christians cannot fight with swords of steel. They cannot rejoice in blood. They cannot, therefore, be the sword in the hand of God..." The government can still fulfill its purpose by other means: "When the Lord has a dirty job, there is no want of dirty undertakers."[21]

Campbell would have no difficulty agreeing with the leading moderate peace activist William Ladd who declared., "The chief end and purpose of government is, to prevent one person from injuring another, so that one may sit under his own vine and fig-tree, with none to molest or make him afraid ... and when disputes arise, so far from leaving each individual to take his own cause in his own hands, governments have provided courts of law to decide the controversy."[22]

## Separation of State from Church

Campbell did not have a philosophy of government that was either clearly defined or extensive. Such as it was, his position arose from late Enlightenment influences and from his understanding of the Bible. He acknowledged a limited role for government in the realms of religion and personal life. Campbell insisted that government had no ecclesiastical responsibility. Any move on the part of the state to intervene in religious affairs, he considered as illegitimate intrusion. He had a basically favorable assessment of the American government. This was due to the fact that it was "purely political."[23]

Campbell's views in this area were largely in keeping with John Locke who also advocated the noninterference in religious matters by governing authorities. Locke defined the commonwealth as "a society of men constituted only for the preserving, and the advancing their own civil interest" with no proper function in the domain of religion.[24] With his belief in tolerance, separation of powers, natural rights and human dignity, Campbell's political thought is reflective of the dominant political philosophy of antebellum America.

The intense aversion that Campbell had to any attempt on the part of the state to exert its power in relation to the church probably went beyond theological or philosophical principles. His mother's family were French Huguenots. When Louis XIV revoked the Edict of Nantes, which granted a degree of religious freedom, the family was forced to flee the country, first to Scotland, then to Ireland.[25] It is very possible that as he was growing up the young Alexander heard stories about this experience with a religiously oppressive state.

Especially during his earlier years Campbell had little confidence in the benevolence of the state in its relation to the church. He thought that governments favored religion to the extent that it served the ends of the state. In an 1828 debate, he quoted Soame Jenyns who stated that in ancient kingdoms leaders manipulated the populace with the belief in rewards and punishment in the afterlife and used the idea of God to give their laws sanction. The state has been most positive toward religion when it has found religion useful to some political purpose.[26]

Campbell believed that since the founding of the church, "the governments of this world have either been directly opposed to it, or, at best, pretended friends; and therefore their influence has always been opposed to the true spirit and genius of the Christian institution."[27] Christians mistakenly believed that the state would genuinely further their cause. The most that could be reasonably expected from the state was "liberty of conscience and protection from violence... till Jesus take to himself his great power, and hurl all these potentates from their thrones and make his cause triumphant."[28]

In his 1830 "Oration in Honor of the Fourth of July," Campbell spoke favorably of the government "in this most favored of all lands" because this "government proposes only to guard the temporal and worldly rights of men." Instead of seeking to promote one faith and inhibit others, the government restricted its efforts exclusively to the concerns of this world. "It permits every man to be of no religion, or of any religion he pleases... Here the affairs of another world are left to themselves."[29] Campbell commended this approach to government. Neither aid nor obstacles should be placed in the way of any religion or the members of any church. Campbell believed the role of government was simply to keep out of all religious matters and insure freedom from persecution.

But he occasionally saw the government inserting itself into religious affairs. In 1843, he was distressed when he learned of the decision of the court in the *Commonwealth vs. William Armstrong* case in Lycoming County, Pennsylvania. Despite the protests of her father, Baptist minister William S. Hall had baptized the seventeen year old daughter of William Armstrong who had already been baptized as a Presbyterian. The father threatened to bring violence upon the minister, which led to the minister seeking legal protection from the court. Judge Ellis Lewis required William Armstrong to post $500 in bond. However, he ruled that the Rev. Hall pay that bond because he had circumvented the father's authority.[30]

Campbell strongly objected to the decision. He declared that the judge's action infringed on the minister's right to proclaim his message and carry out his ministry according to his own convictions. By giving priority to parental authority, the court decision "annihilates personal responsibility, the rights of conscience, and political freedom, at 'one fell swoop.'"[31] A year later, Campbell was pleased to find that in a similar case an opposite decision was issued by another Pennsylvania judge which, Campbell said, "confirmed, in the main, my Review of Judge Lewis' Decision..."[32]

Campbell sought to insure that there was no action by the government that would inhibit the church from carrying out its ministry or from proclaiming the message to which it was committed. Sometimes Campbell's vigilance in identifying and protesting any sign that the state was encroaching upon the domain of the church may have seemed excessive. He went so far as to deny that the governing authorities had the prerogative to grant religious freedom to churches. "The mere asking for toleration recognizes a right which no civil government possesses, and establishes a principle of calamitous consequences."[33]

The government that has the right to extend tolerance to churches, Campbell reasoned, likewise has the right to withhold it if the authorities deem a religious conviction or practice contrary to the majority view or at odds with the aim of the state. Churches, then, would be dependent upon the "intelligence and forbearance" of the government to determine which religions are detrimental to the public interests, and therefore should be opposed, and which should be tolerated. Campbell understood freedom of religion to be a natural right. He declared, "Civil rulers have no right to tolerate nor punish men on account of their opinions in matters of religion."[34]

## Separation of Church from State

If Campbell was wary of the state exerting power over the church, he was equally suspicious of the church seeking to enlist the government for its purposes. His own experience with state-church relations prior to his immigration to the United States made him especially sensitive to any initiatives on the part of a church or its leaders to use the state for its ends. As Campbell interpreted the history of the church, one of the most spiritually and politically destructive developments was the achievement of political power by the church. He wrote:

> In the beginning of the fifth century the Christian religion, had been corrupted into a hierarchy – it had become a state engine; it had, therefore, lost its spirit, its purity, its original power over the empire, conquered its conquerors, and was, beyond doubt, the most puissant element of the new compound.[35]

Campbell wrote in an essay in 1833 that the New Testament assumes Christians will not be in the position to set the course of the state. This is not due merely to the peculiar historical situation of the earliest church, but Campbell believed this to be a result of faithfulness to Christ. A position of dominance in the world – prior to the millennial reign – is contrary to the nature of Christianity. There can be no Christian nation because Christians are not to live by force, but by divine love; in contrast nations depend upon force. Consequently, it is the nature of Christianity to be in a position of political weakness. "Hence," wrote Campbell, "the New Testament is only written and adapted to Christians in a suffering state – not as triumphant, not as having the reins of government in their hands."[36] When Christianity adopts a strategy of power, it becomes other than Christianity. So, Campbell continued, the New Testament being only adapted to Christians in a suffering state, it never can mount the throne, nor become a court religion; and, therefore, any religion called Christian, which has been by law established, has been an impudent imposition or base counterfeit, and not the religion of Jesus Christ.[37]

Christians are spread about in many nations or kingdoms, wrote Campbell, but not one of those nations can rightfully claim to be a Christian nation. Such a claim could be justified only if the nation administered Christ's laws, pledged allegiance to him as the governing authority in all things, and came into being by adopting his constitution.[38] But that could never happen before the millennium. Campbell quoted "one well versed in policies of nations, and in the laws of Christian ethics, and all the writing of the Christian teachers" who made clear the magnitude of the problems of a nation attempting to be governed strictly by the pacifist Christianity of the Bible:

> No nation can be governed by the New Testament alone, nor by the principles which it inculcates; for were we to take Jesus for our King, the Romans or some unchristian kingdom would come and destroy our country and government; for Jesus would not allow us to have a sword or cannon by which to avenge our wrongs – nay, he would have us turn the other cheek when smitten in the face; and when compelled to go one mile, to make it two.[39]

Campbell did not flinch. He refused to compromise the demands of Jesus' teaching or regard them irrelevant in view of the supposed needs of the state. In view of the above citation, he wrote:

> Grant it all its force; and what follows? That no one kingdom can become a kingdom of Jesus Christ until all kingdoms become his; and then it follows that the New Testament is only adapted to Christians while citizens of other kingdoms, being under the governments of those who know not God, and obey not the gospel of his Son.[40]

Campbell not only did not believe the church should have its hands on the reins of government, he held that the Christian religion itself was not adequate for guiding the state in achieving its ends. "The gospel is not a system of morality for the moral improvement of any nation or state."[41] Campbell certainly did not intend to suggest that he did not want the Christian faith to influence the values and policies of the nation. However, to institutionalize and mandate Christian standards for people who were spiritually unprepared, he saw as unconstitutional, unbiblical, and useless. "The church," he wrote, "cannot constitutionally undertake to reform the state. The state, so far as it is not in the church, is composed of men in the flesh – men who live in obedience to all the lusts and passions of the animal man."[42]

Thirteen years later, he stated in similar vein, that Christ "never condescends to legislate for the bodies of men, or their goods and chattels, who withhold from him their conscience and their hearts."[43] The gospel, Campbell believed, must not be used as an instrument to support external coercion, but should be seen as a divine means of persuasion and transformation. Jesus Christ has not made laws for governments.[44] But in various ways Christians and religious organizations had sought to enlist the power of the state or impose sectarian views on the nation. Campbell stood firmly against such activity.

Early in his career Campbell condemned the practice among church groups of adopting resolutions which dealt with government policies. This practice seemed to him to be an expression of the church overstepping its bounds, and interfering with the work of the state. When churches take such action, they obviously declare that they have the authority "to pass resolutions disapprobatory of the proceedings of government, when either their temper or the times require it." Campbell considered this practice a manifestation of "sectarian pride, ambition, and avarice" that threatened the very existence of free and useful institutions.[45]

In the early nineteenth century moral societies became popular as a means for Christians to address social problems. In 1815 the Washington Moral Society was founded by some residents of Washington, Pennsylvania. Its stated purpose was "for the suppression of immorality." The group directed its members "actively to promote the objects of the Association by giving information against anyone known to be guilty of profane swearing, Sabbath-breaking, intoxication, unlawful gaming, keeping a disorderly house, or any other active immorality punished by the Commonwealth."[46] The society started out as a group of informers. They managed to intimidate the citizenry and eventually began to arrest "offenders." Of course they had no legal right to engage in such a practice. In so doing they deprived others of their civil and religious liberties.[47]

In 1820 Campbell, writing under a pseudonym, began to criticize the moral societies in letters to the *Washington Reporter.* After reading his statements, some of the moral and religious leadership in the area declared that he was a "friend to immorality."[48] Campbell wrote again, arguing that the societies were contrary to the faith, the constitution and rationality. "There is no precept or command in the New Testament to compel by civil law, any man who is not a Christian to pay any regard to the Lord's Day, any more than to any other day."[49] He insisted that to coerce people who had no faith into observing Christian practices was at odds with the gospel itself.

Through the years Campbell continued to object to moral societies. In 1837 he explained that "our brethren generally regard the church as the only moral or religious association which they can lawfully patronize because all good works that need to be done can and should be done with and through the church."[50] But early in his career he revealed another motive for opposing these societies. In 1823 he called attention to portions of a tract by the National Tract Society that promoted the idea of a national creed or religious establishment which could be especially helpful during a time of war or crisis. Fearing this might lead to a church-state alliance, he called upon his readers to be wary of these religious leaders and their schemes.[51]

## Christian Selective Engagement

Campbell's assertion that the "church... cannot constitutionally undertake to reform the state" does not mean that Campbell had no Christian political ethic.[52] Rather he believed that it was contrary to the character and purpose of the Church for it to function as a political pressure group in relation to the government. The Church's reforming influence upon the state was through the power of example and the presence of converted individuals, not by means of institutional cohesion. Like other nineteenth century pacifists, he believed when public opinion turned against war, national policy would turn against the practice. Yet he recognized that "all human government presuppose disorder, and? the kingdoms of this world generally have arisen out of confusion and war."[53]

Government and violence are intimately related. Not only do nations arise from deadly conflict, they sustain themselves from internal chaos and collapse by means of violent coercion. Though Campbell utterly repudiated international violence, in the domestic realm he supported police action. However, he offered no practical guidance nor did he ever expressly discuss police action in relation to his commitment to nonviolence in war and self-defense. Yet clearly, he did not regard public life free of spiritual dangers. But he did not advocate the utter repudiation of political involvement. Instead Campbell proposed cautious and selective engagement.

That Campbell had negative things to say about politics, there can be no doubt. This is particularly true after his own experience as a representative at the Virginia Constitutional Congress from October 5, 1829 to January 15, 1830. He saw democracy at work, not as an altruistic endeavor, but as a self-serving scramble for power and privilege, without principled regard for the common good.[54] In 1831 Campbell darkly mused, "The political affairs of the nations are approaching some momentous crisis. The Lord will ere long avenge the infidelity, ingratitude injustice, and blasphemy of the nations."[55] In 1838 Campbell wrote, "Politics are a moral pestilence. The strife of the forum and the fierce debates about... *thiny and miney* – are the scorching wind."[56] On numerous other occasions he expressed concern over the contaminating presence of pride, ambition, and the desire for profit in political life.[57]

Reporting on a 1839 visit to Washington, D.C., Campbell conveyed his impression of the capital. He was struck by the "worldly pomp and splendor" that greeted him. The architecture and gardens were splendid but extravagant. More importantly, he said of the art, "The sculpture and paintings are truly Roman and Pagan, and conspire to prove what little influence the gospel of peace yet exerts over the American people."[58] His overall impression of the city was negative. In a fashion in keeping with his pacifist convictions, he remarked that "our national device, the American Eagle... preaches to the universe that we have more of the spirit of war and of spoil, than of the peaceful Dove in our Constitution."[59]

Still, despite his occasional displeasure, Campbell did not call for withdrawal from public life. Less than a year after the New England Non-Resistance Society was formed, Campbell received a letter from M. Winans of Jamestown, Ohio inquiring about "this new doctrine?called the doctrine of 'non-resistance.'" He stated that "some honest-hearted well-meaning men amongst us" had concluded that the Scriptures forbid Christians from having any political role. They could not hold an office in government. Even voting is prohibited by the gospel, according to them, wrote Winans. This withdrawal from governments is essential for true Christianity and the reception of solution, its advocates claimed.[60]

The answer, published in the *Millennial Harbinger*, was written by his father Thomas but was in harmony with the views of Alexander. The issues of voting and office holding are not directly addressed. However, he does state that nonresistance "is certainly unscriptural," and that obedience to the biblical message does not interfere with political duties.[61] Campbell does not write so much to urge politics involvement as to oppose anything that smacks of anarchy. Obedience to governing authorities – except in rare instances of rebellion against God's command – is biblically mandated. Political engagement is permitted. But here Campbell certainly does not urge doing any more than is necessary to comply with the law.

"Ought Christians to take an active part in politics?" Alexander Campbell asked in 1840. That year the presidential campaign was bitter and Campbell found contention "from the palace to the meanest wigwam." Everywhere people were "agitated by this fierce demon of discord." Campbell could not see enough good in choosing one candidate over another to outweigh the evil of animosity and division that pervaded both the church and the country. In view of the situation, he answered that Christians should not be actively involved in politics. "One of my reasons is American politics are full of avarice and ambition. They are national and mammoth forms of pride and cupidity; or they are a concentration of selfishness."[62]

But Campbell's judgment of the 1840 political scene was not necessarily his assessment of politics at all times and places. When he asked whether Christians ought to be involved in politics, he qualified the question by adding, "in the present politics of this country." He observed, "The present politics of this country are more purely mercenary than any other politics in any other country, or the former politics of our own country."[63] He believed that the particular circumstances at that time made it expedient for Christians to temporarily withdraw from the political process.

Campbell saw politicians preoccupied with the passion for self-gain, unscrupulous with the truth and incessantly self-important. And so he declared, "The spirit of politicians and the spirit of God are as antagonistic as flesh and spirit, as hatred and love, as heaven and hell; and he that would faithfully and truly serve the one, must abjure all allegiance to the other."[64] He went on to say of Christians, "Would to God that they would set their affections on the politics of heaven, and leave the politics of earth to those who cannot soar above the Allegheny Mountains."[65]

of the disparaging things Campbell said of politics possibly emerged out of disgust at the pride of politicians who had a bloated sense of their vocation.[66] But in part his judgment that the workings of government are of relatively little importance was due to the comparatively great importance he saw in the work of God's kingdom. He wrote, "The great capitals of earth – the centers of nations and empires – with all their thrones, their halls legislative, judiciary and executive, are but for the present scaffolding of humanity, while the Christian temple – that building of God's own Son – is in progress of erection."[67] Campbell reminded his readers that the realms of this world will pass away but the realm of God is eternal.

Campbell could say, "I know nothing more antipodal to the gospel than politics," because of the self-centered, antagonistic power struggle between politicians. Yet Campbell does concede "there have been a few statesmen who have been devoted to religion, and some to Christianity."[68] He names several examples through the centuries, being careful to indicate they were a small minority. The only contemporary on his honor-roll of Christian politicians was the pacifist Soame Jenyns of the English Parliament. "Still it is about as hard for a Christian man to please unchristian constituents," Campbell insisted, "as it is for any one to serve God and Mammon. The true politician rises by descending to cater for the lusts and passions of men."[69] So in the strictest sense, Campbell did not hold participation in political office to be absolutely wrong, but in most cases ill advised. Few who attempt it, he believed, manage to be good politicians and faithful Christians.

In keeping with his stress upon the unity of the church, Campbell himself avoided partisan politics. When he was asked in 1846 about his political commitments, he answered that parties and politicians had little of his loyalty but "there were certain principles and policies to which I sometimes gave my suffrage."[70] It was for "principles and policies" rather than partisan interests that led Campbell to be a delegate at the Virginia Constitutional Congress. He believed the formation of a constitution was "one of the most grave and solemn of all political matters, and not like the ordinary affairs of legislation."[71]

## Positive Shift

In 1847 Campbell made a trip to England and Europe during which he had an opportunity to visit Parliament. This occasion seems to have provided a turning point in his attitude toward the government. While there he was pleased to hear speeches by several statesmen, including Lord Brougham and the Duke of Wellington, and the experience apparently deepened his appreciation for the United States and its political system.

Reflecting on the addresses he heard in Parliament, he wrote, "The whole House of Lords, Bishops, and all... are in no intellectual endowments superior to a Virginia House of Delegates, an Ohio Senate, or any other deliberative body elected by any sovereign State of the American Union."[72] Earlier that same year he praised the United States for its numerous positive qualities and celebrated its government as "the most rational, equitable, and free, ever vouchsafed to man."[73]

After returning to America, Campbell again visited Washington, D.C. His report stands in sharp contrast to the reflections he offered of his tour of the capital eight years earlier. He favorably compared the state buildings to "any capital, parliament, court, or legislative hall in Europe."[74] This time he made no complaint of the influence of paganism on the art or architecture. Nor did he rail against the politicians and declare their activity in contradiction to the spirit of the gospel as he had on earlier occasions. In fact, he declared that some of the elected representatives were equal in statesmanship to political leaders anywhere in the world.[75]

Actually Campbell's increasingly friendly attitude toward politics began even before his trip to England and Europe.[76] He became more positive in the mid-1840's. This outlook continued until he again became disillusioned as the Civil War approached. His position is well-summarized in his own words: "While I adjure, *ex animo*, all politico-ecclesiastical systems, all combinations of politics and religion, all confederative unions of church and state, I nevertheless believe that the excellency of the American system of society and government consists in its nearer approach to Christianity than that of any other national polity in the world."[77]

Though he did not do so often, Campbell did occasionally make a point of urging Christians to vote on specified policies. In this he stands in sharp contrast to the Non-Resistants. He encouraged political support for common school education in a 1841 address, though he made no claim of representing ***the*** Christian position on the issue.[78] In discussing the tactics of the abolitionists, which he held in disfavor, he suggested that Christians ought to make their will about slavery known with their votes. "The laws sustain it," he wrote, "A Christian may, indeed, seek by his vote to have it annihilated or modified."[79]

That same year Campbell reminded his readers that by using their vote they could change the slave laws of the nation.[80] Never did Campbell suggest neglecting their political right to vote to be a spiritual behavior. Though not throwing his support to a particular party or politician, he told his readers, "Vote like Christians."[81] Yet he did little to explain what that might mean in practice.

Why was Campbell negative toward political involvement to the extent that he was? Was it because of a sectarian impulse to withdraw from society? Was his pacifism but one expression of that impulse? His lack of consistency in his actions and teachings about the state suggest that wholesale withdrawal was not his aim. There must be a better explanation. George Richard Phillips maintains that the reason lies with Campbell's Lockian concern for the elimination of ecclesiastical dominance of the state.[82] It is very likely that is part of the reason, but not all of it.

Campbell's own less than happy participation in the Virginia Constitutional Congress was probably a factor. This experience led him to view politicians as selfish and not truly in pursuit of the common good. Consequently, he questioned whether politics was a vocation suitable for Christians. Further, his observance of divisive and bitter political campaigns, political rhetoric without practical results, and unscrupulous, self-serving politicians played a role in forming his attitude. In addition to this, Campbell's priority on church unity led him to urge Christians to be careful not to engage in divisive political affairs. Campbell was thoroughly convinced that the destiny of the world rested, not with the outcome of national or international politics, but with the faithful practice of the church. Hence, he opposed anything that might hinder the church in its work.

It appears that the one area from which Campbell certainly did advocate withdrawal from public life was the military. Since the purpose of the military was to prepare for, and when called upon to do so, participate in war, Campbell saw no place in it for Christians. But with this exception, his pacifist convictions did not lead him to promote utter disengagement from the affairs of the state. The position he adopted was not greatly unlike that of many moderate pacifists within the American Peace Society.

## Notes

1. Peter Brock, *Radical Pacifists in Antebellum America* (Princeton: Princeton University Press, 1968), 78.
2. Valarie H. Ziegler, *The Advocates of Peace in Antebellum America* (Bloomington, IN:

Indiana University Press, 1992), 23.
3. ibid., 33f.
4. Brock, op. cit., 39.
5. ibid., 41.
6. ibid., 57f.
7. Thomas Upham, *The Manual of Peace: Exhibiting the Evils and Remedies of War* (Boston: American Peace Society, 1842), 267.
8. William Lloyd Garrison, *Selections From the Writings and Speeches of William Lloyd Garrison* (Boston: R.F. Wallcut, 1852), 97.
9. ibid., 93.
10. ibid., 94.
11. Brock, op. cit., 184.
12. Roland Bainton "Alexander Campbell and the Social Order," in *The Sage of Bethany* (The Bethany Press, St. Louis, MO, 1960), 122.
13. Alexander Campbell, *Popular Lectures and Addresses* (Philadelphia: James Challen & Son, 1863), 374.
14. Alexander Campbell, *The Christian System* (Nashville: Gospel Advocate, 1964), 125.
15. *Millennial Harbinger*, 1845. 316.
16. ibid., 1846, 142-143.
17. ibid., 1851, 389.
18. ibid., 1846, 123.
19. ibid., 124.
20. ibid., 1845, 316.
21. ibid., 1835, 145-146.
22. William Ladd, *An Essay On A Congress of Nations* (Boston: American Peace Society, 1840), 3.
23. *Millennial Harbinger*, 1830, 305.
24. John Locke, *Four Letters on Tolerance* (London: Alexander Murray, 1820), 5.
25. Robert Richardson, *Memoirs of Alexander Campbell*, I (Philadelphia: J.B. Lippencott & Co., 1868), 21.
26. Alexander Campbell and Robert Owen, *The Evidences of Christianity: A Debate* (Nashville: McQuiddy Publishing Co., 1957), 405.
27. *The Christian System*, 135.
28. ibid.
29. *Millennial Harbinger*, 1830, 305.
30. ibid., 1843, 98ff.
31. ibid., 109.
32. ibid., 1844, 238.
33. *The Christian Baptist*, III, 204.
34. ibid., 205.
35. Alexander Campbell, *Popular Lectures and Addresses*, 52.
36. *Millennial Harbinger*, 1833, 120.
37. ibid.
38. ibid.
39. ibid.
40. ibid.

41. ibid., 1845, 238.
42. ibid.
43. ibid., 108.
44. *Popular Lectures and Addresses*, 361.
45. *The Christian Baptist*, II, 143.
46. Richardson, I, op. cit., 517.
47. Lunger, op. cit., 45.
48. Richardson, op. cit., 523.
49. ibid.
50. *Millennial Harbinger*, 1837, 271.
51. *The Christian Baptist*, III, 60-64.
52. ibid., 36f.
53. *The Christian System*, 124.
54. On Campbell's experience at the Virginia Constitutional Convention, see Lunger, chapter seven, 75-104.
55. *Millennial Harbinger*, 1831, 211.
56. ibid., 1838, 474. Emphasis his.
57. ibid., 1833, 3, 12, 120f.
58. ibid., 1839, 7f.
59. ibid., 8.
60. ibid., 1839, 576.
61. ibid.
62. *Millennial Harbinger*, 1840, 414.
63. ibid.
64. ibid., 415.
65. ibid.
66. *Millennial Harbinger*, 1838, 3.
67. *Popular Lectures and Addresses*, 521.
68. *Millennial Harbinger*, 1845, 316.
69. ibid.
70. *Millennial Harbinger*, 1846, 4.
71. Richardson, II, op. cit., 319f.
72. *Millennial Harbinger*, 1847, 378.
73. ibid., 431f.
74. *Millennial Harbinger*, 1850, 407.
75. ibid.
76. *Millennial Harbinger*, 1845, 316.
77. ibid., 1853, 487f. This is not a reversal of Campbell's previous thinking nor, as Lunger proposed, a development from a sect type ecclesiology to a denominational ecclesiology. However, there are differences of emphasis in his writing at different points in his career. Still, as early as 1830 he could write, "*The light which shines from our political institutions will penetrate even the dungeons of European despots for the genius of our Government is the genius of universal emancipation! Nothing can resist the political influence of a great nation, enjoying our great political advantages if she walks worthy of them.*" *Popular Lectures and Addresses*, 374.

## Chapter 6

# War, Slavery and Civil Disobedience

Since Alexander Campbell taught that Christians should not fight in wars or serve in the military, he potentially put his followers on a collision course with the authority of the state. If legally compelled to bear arms to pursue the aims or defend the interests of the nation, they could either be forced to betray their pacifist conviction and obey the state, or disobey the laws of the land and stay true to their commitment to nonviolence. This problem did not go unaddressed by Campbell. On more than one occasion he discussed the prospect of disobeying the state for the sake of conscience, the practice now called civil disobedience.

### Conflict with Non-Resistants

The first time the matter of civil disobedience was discussed in the pages of the *Millennial Harbinger* at any length was in response to the 1839 letter Campbell received from M. Winans regarding his encounter with some Garrisonian non-resistants.[1] He said that the men conceded that Christians are to be subject to "the powers that be," that is the governing authorities. However, said Winans, the non-resistants distinguished two types of subjection or obedience to the powers, active and passive. Active obedience is when one simply followed the dictates of the authorities. Passive obedience is "the obedience of disobedience." In other words, it is noncompliance to the law along with the willingness to "suffer the penalty of disobedience." The only specific example he cited is when "the Christian is commanded to muster or march in the army, he disobeys the command, but pays the fine imposed on him for disobedience." This viewpoint, according to its advocates, wrote Winans, "is supposed to be fully taught in the Lord's Sermon on the Mount."[2]

The responsibility for answering the letter in the *Millennial Harbinger* fell to Alexander Campbell's father, Thomas. There is, however, no evidence of significant disagreement between father and son. Thomas Campbell's answer sounded very much like the response the more conservative and moderate members of the American Peace Society offered to the non-resistants. He claimed that Christians have two lines of duty. As individuals, they are to refrain from retaliation or even self-defense. He cited numerous passages of scripture in both New and Old Testaments in support of the position that Christians are to love and not resist evil by force. However, he maintained, "all this [is] without any interference with our political duties; as the subjects of civil government."[3]

He differentiated between personal duties and public responsibilities in a manner reminiscent of Martin Luther's notion of the two kingdoms. The distinction, he held, was biblical: "For he that said, 'Resist not evil'; also said, (Matt. xxii.21.,) 'Render to Cesar (sic) the things that are Cesar's.'" He then referred to several other passages of scripture dealing with honoring and obeying those in authority (Rom. 13:1-7; Tit. 3:1; I Pet. 2:13-17). In the end, he set a limit on the obedience Christians are permitted to offer to the government saying that "our civil obligations do not bind us to do anything that the Lord has forbid us to do. For while we are to render to Cesar the things that are Cesar's, we must also render to God the things that are God's."[4]

This response was obviously quite conservative, reflecting great reluctance to act contrary to the dictates of the governing authorities. The scriptures the elder Campbell proffered to make his point were among the same ones used by his son, Alexander, to echo that point years later. Those of non-resistant convictions were very familiar with the biblical case used against their position. They could not avoid dealing with such passages of scripture as Romans 13: 1-7, which were so often held before them by their opponents. Garrison called those verses, "frowning Gibraltar, inaccessible by sea and land, filled with troops and all warlike instruments, and able to vanquish every assailing force."[5]

Still Garrison denied that these verses in fact undermine the non-resistant position. St. Paul and the Christians of the first century renounced the use of violence yet gave a conditional recognition of the governing powers within God's structure of order. That conditional recognition did not entail compliance with the government in any matter which would lend support to an injustice or further violence. Hence, sweeping allegiance to the governing powers cannot be justified on Christian principles, claimed Garrison. Pharaoh,

Nebuchadnezzar and Caesar all served as God's instruments after a fashion yet no follower of Christ could be warranted pledging loyalty to such rulers and sharing the use of the sword.[6]

Campbell's literalistic reading of Romans 13 and other portions of scripture left him predisposed to oppose civil disobedience. The non-resistants like Garrison were temperamentally and ideologically prone to engage in such actions. Still in spite of the high wall Campbell erected in defense of obedience to the "powers that be," he did build into it one small but important window. The governing authorities were not to be obeyed in any matter that was contrary to the explicit will of God as expressed in the New Testament. The conflict Campbell had with the non-resistants – many of whom were also abolitionists – was regarding precisely what God had in fact forbidden. They largely agreed on the matter of war; their conflict however was on other issues.

## An Influential Contemporary

Among nineteenth century thinkers who discussed civil disobedience and were likely to have influenced Campbell was Dr. Francis Wayland, a Baptist minister, leading moral philosopher and president of Brown University. Wayland had written an extremely popular text on moral philosophy which sold over two hundred thousand copies. It was used in classes by Campbell at Bethany College. The Millennial Harbinger frequently contained quotes from and references to Wayland. In many ways Campbell's thought was similar to that of the philosopher. Wayland was a part of a school of thought known as Academic Orthodoxy. Thinkers of this school were not staid conservatives but, according to Edward Maddox, they often "really represented the liberal thrust of Protestant Christianity."[7] They were intellectual heirs of John Locke and were greatly influenced by the Scottish realists, particularly Thomas Reid and Dugald Steward.

Wayland was a vice-president of the American Peace Society by the late 1830's and from 1854-1861 he served as its president.[8] It was a boost to the respectability of the peace movement that one as highly regarded as Wayland came out in support of absolute pacifism.[9] He rejected the view that the moral standards which apply to individual behavior are not applicable to nations. According to Wayland "men connected in societies are under the same moral law as individuals." Retaliation was not permitted to individuals and so was also forbidden to nations. "Hence, it would seem that all wars are contrary to the revealed will of God, and that the individual has no right to commit to society, nor society to commit to government, the power to declare war...God commands us to love every man, alien or citizen, Samaritan or Jew, as ourselves; and the act neither of society nor of government can render it our duty to violate this command."[10]

In general Wayland, like Campbell, believed that Christian citizens were obligated to obey all laws put in place by the governing authorities. A law could not be ignored simply because it is "unwise or inexpedient."[11] Each person did not have a right to pick and choose among laws, obeying only those which pleased them, declared Wayland. All citizens must comply with the laws lest there be social chaos. However, he acknowledged that there are occasions when government goes beyond its properly constituted limits in the establishment of laws. In such cases what, he asked, is the duty of the individual?[12]

In answer to his own question, Wayland offered three possibilities. First, one could passively obey the government though the law be unrighteous. Wayland rejected that option as irresponsible. Second, resistance by force could be attempted, using physical violence if necessary. However, he deemed such behavior was unacceptable. It would "dissolve the social fabric" and lead to destruction and demoralization, cautioned Wayland. The third possible course of action he proposed he called "suffering in the cause of right." Citizens would refuse to comply with the morally dubious law but nonviolently submit to the punishment meted out by the authorities. Wayland considered this response the most appropriate because it appealed to the reason and conscience of others. Further, he claimed that "experience has shown that the cause of civil liberty has always gained more by martyrdom than by war."[13]

When the United States entered into war with Mexico, Wayland urged Christians to resist. In a powerful series of sermons in Brown University chapel, he spoke on "The Duty of Obedience to the Civil Magistrate." The series might better have been named "The Duty of Disobedience to the Civil Magistrate." Though he never expressly mentioned the war, it was clearly understood as the occasion for the sermons. He maintained that when the magistrate commands people to do something that is wrong, his words should be regarded as having no more authority than the command of any other person who is wrong. If punishment comes for resisting the command, so be it. The nation that commands its people to do something contrary to the Gospel of Jesus Christ forfeits the right to obedience, declared Wayland. "[What] is the will of a nation in comparison with the command of Almighty God, and what can be the measure of that impiety which exclaims, 'our country, whether right or wrong,' that is, our country in defiance of the Eternal One himself."[14]

The disobedience Wayland urged in the face of the war with Mexico certainly fit through the window in Campbell's wall of civil disobedience. Both men condemned the war by laying out principles intended to cause Christians to see that support of the war was incompatible with faithfulness to Christ rather than by denouncing the particular war at hand.[15] But they had something else in common as well, at least through the 1830's. Both men regarded slavery as a deplorable evil yet they opposed the methods of abolitionists.

Wayland, like Campbell, was hesitant to claim that getting rid of slavery was a moral imperative and both men believed that immediate emancipation of slaves would be disastrous for the slaves since they were not accustomed to self-government.[16] Both men thought moral reasoning and persuasion would eventually lead Southerners to voluntarily end slavery. However, as the 1840's progressed, Wayland became more favorable toward the abolitionists. When the Fugitive Slave Law was enacted, he renounced it as immoral and unworthy of support. By the time the Civil War began, Wayland had come to offer support for defensive wars in certain circumstances, as did most other peace advocates.[17] Campbell at no point would support civil disobedience to end slavery and throughout the war between North and South he maintained his position as an absolute pacifist.

## Position on Slavery

At different points through the years, Campbell was accused of being both an abolitionist and pro-slavery. Sometimes he was condemned for both positions at the same time. These accusations are not entirely surprising. In the first issue of *The Christian Baptist*, among the things he declared as incompatible with true Christianity was the Christian support of slavery, "a system of the most cruel oppression," in which "might gives right."[18] In the early 1830's he called slavery, "that largest and blackest blot upon our national escutcheon, that many-headed monster... whose breath pollutes and poisons everything within its influence."[19] He supported the idea of using federal money to buy slaves and to help them colonize a portion of Africa or some unpopulated area in the Americas.[20] This idea was in currency among some of the more moderate and conservative reformers at the time.

However, when abolitionists called for the immediate liberation of all slaves and scathingly denounced the Southern slave owners as sinners in need of repentance, Campbell called for restraint. In part this was due to his concern over the bloodshed he anticipated if the more radical solution of the forcible release of the slaves was pursued. Campbell was afraid that insofar as the abolitionists were concerned, the slavery issue could be discussed only "by the light of burning palaces, cities and temples, amidst the roar of cannon, the clangor of trumpets, the shrieks of dying myriads... and the agonizing throes of the last and best republic on earth."[21] Campbell found abolitionists inflexible, self-righteous and judgmental.

While Campbell wanted to see the end of slavery, he also wanted to preserve the unity of both nation and church. He was in no sympathy with those who were heedless of the broader consequences in their quest for the liberation of the slaves. Campbell believed slavery to be a great evil, but he would not call it a sin, as did the abolitionists.[22] As an institution slavery could be justified by both the New Testament and Old Testament, contended Campbell. Within the Bible, however, there is much guidance offered to regulate the relationship between slave and master which should be followed.[23] But the practice of slavery itself was not expressly condemned.

Still, Campbell was careful not to equate slavery in the New Testament with the slavery practiced in the American South. "When I affirm that the New Testament recognizes without censure the relation of master and slave, I do not say that it sanctions the legalized treatment of either master or slaves according to the American or any other code."[24] Campbell continued to oppose slavery, but called for moderation, patience, and cooperation. He stood against those in the church who wanted to disfellowship all slave owners.[25] At the same time he urged the elders of the churches to discipline any master whose slaves were abused and treated unfairly.[26] He believed that whatever was done with slavery, it was imperative to "preserve unity of spirit among Christians of the South and of the North."[27]

Campbell's strongest, most compelling anti-slavery declaration came in 1849 at a time when the state of Kentucky called a constitutional convention to address the slave question. Campbell composed a tract to the people of Kentucky urging them to put an end to slavery. He wrote "not as a citizen of Virginia, nor as a citizen of Kentucky, but as a citizen of the world and a member of Christ's church." He declared that the "emancipation of masters is full as much an object near to my heart as the emancipation of slaves."[28] Campbell saw the effects of slavery as detrimental to all who are touched by it. He wrote, "The intercourse between a master and a slave, however kind and generous the former, and however pliant and obedient the latter, is, on the one side, essentially dogmatical, absolute, and lordly, on the other side, cringing, servile and abject."[29] He called upon his readers to lift up their voices and cast their votes against slavery. Later, when a *Millennial Harbinger* subscriber complained about the tract to Kentucky, Campbell replied, "that slavery, as established by our laws, is [not] either in harmony with the Bible, or the spirit of this age, or the progress of society."[30]

## Fugitive Slave Law

Consistently Campbell was an advocate of social and political change by means of legal process. When the Fugitive Slave Law was passed in 1850 the issue of the extent to which the governing authorities should be obeyed demanded attention as never before during Campbell's life. Because of the disruptive activity of abolitionists in earlier years, Campbell had already raised the question, "How far ought we to obey and submit to our political institutions – and rulers – or what is the extent of our allegiance to civil government?"[31]

More than once he gave his answer. In 1845 he wrote that as long as slavery was legal, it was "the duty of every Christian man to respect it and to offer no violence." But could nonviolent resistance to slavery be sanctioned? Campbell said no. He insisted that no person could as a citizen or a Christian, "violate or tempt others to violate existing laws without offending his Lord and becoming obnoxious to his displeasure."[32] Campbell seemed to place the obligation to obey the laws of the land over the need to alleviate the suffering of those being oppressed. His contention was that there was a legal means of addressing slavery. Consequently, illegal direct action tactics were both wrong and unnecessary. The legal means was explicitly rejected by the radical pacifists or non-resistants, many of whom were abolitionists. Campbell looked upon their strategy as representing a will to disrupt society.

Later in 1845, Campbell again spoke to the issue of disobedience to the law for conscience's sake. He declared that the Christian must respect and not resist any laws that the state enacts, regardless if they are abstractly right or wrong, so long as the law does not require behavior condemned in scripture. Since "nothing is tolerated in the New Testament that is sinful, immoral, or in tendency injurious," all laws not contrary to the New Testament, however offensive to one's sense of reason, should be supported by any, "law-abiding Christian."[33] Campbell persisted in dealing with slavery in abstract or biblical terms rather than examining the particular practice of slavery found in the nineteenth century American South. Too often he discussed the matter as a topic of biblical interpretation rather than as a matter of contemporary injustice.

A Christian has no right, according to Campbell, to be ruled by his or her opinions or convictions if doing so would entail "any violence to the law, or to aid in the violation of them." He maintained the Christian must "'be subject to every ordinance of man,' and to 'the powers that be, because they are ordained of God,' saith the eternal and almighty King. These views, as it appears to me, are so scripturally and rationally obvious as to commend themselves to the unsophisticated good sense of any Christian and intelligent community."[34]

These same themes were picked up again and dealt with in more depth in 1851 after the Fugitive Slave Law had stirred considerable debate throughout the country. Campbell noted that the Law was being condemned as immoral and unconstitutional in large political and religious gatherings in the North. People were being encouraged by abolitionists, including some ministers, to resist its dictates. Campbell was distressed that "any one well-instructed in the Christian religion could recommend violence, or insubordination to a law passed by a Congress that merely represents and reflects the will of the sovereign people."[35] Over against the abolitionists, Campbell defended the constitutionality of the Fugitive Slave Law. In so doing he employed arguments used by pro-slavery forces, even though he himself had opposed slavery. For instance, he cited the tenth commandment of the Sinai Code: "Thou shalt not covet thy neighbor's... man servant, nor his maid servant... nor anything that is thy neighbor's property." This commandment, he claimed, proved a "divine recognition... of one man having a rightful property in another."[36]

As he had on previous occasions, Campbell appealed to Romans 13:1-7 and I Peter 2:13-18 to call upon his readers to submit to "the higher powers" and "every ordinance" for "the Lord's sake." He cited the examples of Paul returning the slave Onesimus to his master and of the runaway slave Hagar being told by an angel to return to her mistress.[37] He held that it was illegitimate for the resisters of the Fugitive Slave Law to appeal to a "higher law" for in this matter none existed. "In the affairs of this life – in all temporal and earthly matters – the civil law, the social compact, is our rule of action."[38]

Some people had expressed concern for slaves who may be returned to harsh and cruel masters. Campbell denied that the Christian had any responsibility for what happened to the slave after he or she was turned back over to the master. The responsibility would be entirely that of the slave owner. He acknowledged the possibility that some of the masters would be cruel to the returned slaves. His response was, "Have the laws of God or of the state, constituted each and every citizen such a judge?"[39] When some of his readers reacted to his articles by saying that the Golden Rule made it impossible "to sustain or comply with the requisitions of the Fugitive Slave Law," he side-stepped the argument. Campbell ignored the spirit of the Golden Rule and simply asserted that the Bible is "the only infallible standard by which all the relations of human life, and all the duties and obligations growing out of them, are to be adjudicated."[40] When he himself used the Golden Rule in connection with the practice of slavery, he claimed that a master should do "to others as they would, ***in similar circumstances***, have others do to themselves," thereby severely qualifying its relevance of the Rule.[41]

In his determination to uphold the Christian duty to obey governing authorities, Campbell seemed less than sensitive to those upon whom the laws rested most heavily. However, he did interpret the Fugitive Slave Law in a way that was strikingly lenient. He claimed that the law did not inhibit expressions of Christian love by threatening civil penalties for showing acts of kindness to runaway slaves. Feeding, clothing, providing lodging or giving directions to one suspected to be a slave in flight was not forbidden, according to Campbell.[42] Slaves could legally be aided in a large number of ways.

Actually, he noted, the law stated only that one could not harbor or conceal the slave "so as to prevent the discovery and arrest of such person after notice or knowledge of the fact that such person is a fugitive from service or labor aforesaid." Campbell maintained that unless legal notice and knowledge asserted that the fugitive was a slave, the law hindered no one from offering whatever help they desired. Furthermore, unless one attempted to "harbor or conceal him, so as to prevent discovery" the law is not relevant.[43] By this rendering of the law Campbell turns it into a "don't ask, don't tell" policy. In view of such an inventive legal interpretation, one author commented, "This raises some questions about Campbell's sincerity concerning the enforcement of the law. Such an interpretation would allow the abolitionists to aid an escaping slave over the underground railroad, and stay within the law."[44]

A considerable number of the Disciples in the North had no intention of complying with the dictates of the Fugitive Slave Law no matter how Campbell interpreted it. He wrote early in 1851 that the responses from the North he had received to his position ran about half pro, half con. On the con side were "some very conscientious brethren" in Berrien, Michigan. In full assembly the members of that congregation unanimously resolved:

> 1. That Christians are required by their Lord and Master to yield a cheerful obedience to the 'powers that be,' provided their laws do not contravene the 'higher law.'
> 2. That the Fugitive Slave Law, passed by Congress at its last session, does obviously conflict with the Divine Law in several particulars.
> 3. That it is not only not the duty of Christians to obey the sa'd law, but a positive dereliction of duty to their Divine Master, to regard it as of any authority over them.
> 4. That choosing to 'obey God rather than man,' we will not assist the master in recapturing 'the servant that has escaped from his master,' but will feed the poor panting fugitive, and point him to the North Star, abiding the penalty of the law.
> 5. That we have long borne with slavery, for the sake of the Union, as Christians ought to do; but when called upon to aid and abet in perpetuating the institution, we beg to be excused.
> 6. That as citizens of the United States, we will petition our National Legislature for the immediate and unconditional repeal of this oppressive law, so very repugnant to a radical principle of our political *magna charta* – liberty of conscience.
> 7. That we will discountenance all violent measures of opposition to the said law, or to any other, but will pray for our rulers, and suffer persecution at their hands with patience and forbearance, giving glory to the Lord of all.[45]

Two additional articles of the resolution expressed the intent to send the document to the president of the United States and to several Christian publications in addition to the *Millennial Harbinger*, encouraging other church members to suffer for what is right.

The most powerful response to Campbell's position came from Ohio minister and founder of the *Christian Standard* magazine, Isaac Errett. He produced a number of biblical examples of God's people resisting the civil authorities. Then he showed the inadequacy of Campbell's own interpretation of the cases of Onesimus and Hagar and indicated other weaknesses in his arguments from scripture. Finally Errett turned one of Campbell's arguments back on him. Early in 1851 Campbell had appealed to the "immortal Washington" in an attempt to bolster his case for obeying the civil authorities.[46] Taking aim at Campbell's pacifist conviction Errett asked, did not the "immortal Washington" also "lead armies to fight? Is that any argument for war?" Errett went on to say, "if the heritage of freedom we enjoy was... 'purchased with the life-blood of the good and the brave,' what kind of argument does that furnish for the 'absolute supremacy of the law?' And how can we, in turn, bequeath inviolate to our descendants, that heritage, by tamely... submitting to, unrighteous and oppressive laws?"[47]

In his determined defense of full compliance with the law, Campbell violated his own dispensational principles of biblical interpretation. He chose biblicist rigidity over the spirit of the scripture teachings, especially evident with his use of the Golden Rule. In the end, he opted for law and order over justice. How ironic it seems – at least from a twenty-first century perspective – that the next year as he was singing the praises of Protestantism before the Philo-Literary Society of Canonsburg College in Pennsylvania, Campbell declared, "There is a moral heroism in non-conformity to unjust laws and unholy requirements."[48]

## War Resistance

In regard to the obligation Christians have to submit to the governing powers, Campbell wanted people to know that "American slavery and...war ... are very different subjects."[49] The vigor with which he defended the obligation of Christians to obey the law in regard to the return of escaped slaves was absent when he spoke of war. Yet perhaps it was not so strange. The same biblicism that led him to affirm the institution of slavery – but not the American practice of it – led him to denounce war. Since slavery was present and uncondemned in both Old and New Testament, he could not condone Christians taking the law into their own hands to oppose it. But since war and hatred were clearly condemned in the New Testament, he did not hesitate to advocate disobedience to the governing authorities in order to withhold support for war.

Support of war by the church and its clergy was considered by Campbell as "desecrating the religion of the Prince of Peace."[50] The practice of war was regarded by him as utterly at odds with the work of the church. Thus the church could offer none of its resources, including its members, to help in war efforts. In his "Address on War" Campbell reminded his audience that "civil magistrates were God's ministers to the Christian 'for good.'" That being the case, Christians are obligated to "render to Caesar what is Caesar's and to God what is God's," which included "to reverence, honor, and support the civil magistrate; and, when necessary, to claim his protection."[51]

But when it came to the business of war, Campbell saw a clear limit to the legitimate authority of the governing powers. Obedience to the state must end, he believed, when preparation for war begins. Christians must not cooperate. "On the contrary, [Christians] were to live peaceably with all men to the full extent of their power."[52] The only warfare a Christian was to engage in was spiritual warfare; the only armaments fitting for the Christian soldier were spiritual armaments, all of which were unsuitable for battles of blood and steel engaged in by the warriors of this world.

Campbell wrote that he considered the "great question" to be, "Can an individual, not a public functionary, morally do that in obedience to his government which he cannot do in his own case?"[53] He answered that question by telling a story. Suppose, he said, a man with servants had a conflict with his neighbor whom he believed had taken a part of his land. The neighbor refuses to relinquish the land. In response the first man sets out to retake his property. He tells his servants to destroy all the improvements the trespassing neighbor made on the disputed territory and to fire weapons at that neighbor, his family and his servants. The first man's servants obey and kill several of the others. They are arrested and brought to trial.

The attorney of the first man's servants, in arguing on their behalf, maintains their innocence. The servants were obligated to obey the orders of their master, insists the attorney. To bolster his claim, he quotes from the Bible: "Servants, obey in all things your masters according to the flesh." But, says

Campbell, the prosecutor would surely show that "all things" means "all things lawful" for this obedience is supposed to be "as the servants of Christ, doing the will of God from the heart." Certainly the servants would be held accountable and jury and judge would condemn them as guilty of murder.[54]

Drawing the connection, Campbell argued that Christian citizens, though politically inferior to the governing authorities of the state, are accountable and cannot of right obey the government in anything that is not right according to the scriptures. Sharpening his point further, Campbell insisted, "that a Christian man can never, of right, be compelled to do that for the state, in defense of state's rights, which he cannot of right do for himself in defense of his personal rights."[55] The Christian who is commanded to love his neighbor as he loves himself is not commanded to love the state, a king, or anyone more than he loves or serves himself. Hence, Campbell concluded, unless the Christian can go to war for him or herself, the Christian is not justified in going to war for the state.[56]

In short, it could be said that, on the one hand, Campbell opposed disobeying the governing authorities in the case of the Fugitive Slave Law because obeying that law did not require Christians to do anything clearly condemned in scripture. On the other hand, Christians should disobey the state when called to war because war is at odds with the teaching of the New Testament. It is arguable that in both cases Campbell took the position he did – at least in part – because of his pacifism. It was concern over the uncompromising radical nature of the abolitionists and the likely response of the South that made him moderate his own outspoken condemnation of slavery. He believed that the abolitionists' attitudes and tactics would probably lead to war.[57] In response he took a more conciliatory stance, encouraging patience, obedience to the laws, reform rather than revolution, and unity in both church and nation. While such an approach would delay freeing the slaves, it would also, he thought, help avoid even greater evil and suffering – war.

Unfortunately Campbell's worst fears were realized. In 1861 he found himself lamenting, "Civilized America! Civilized United States! Boasting of a humane and Christian paternity and fraternity, unsheathing your swords, discharging your cannon, boasting of your heathen brutality, gluttonously satiating your furious appetites for fraternal blood, caps the climax of all human inconsistencies inscribed on the blurred and moth eaten pages of time in all its records."[58]

# Notes

1. *Millennial Harbinger*, (1839), 575f.
2. ibid.
3. ibid., 576.
4. ibid., 577.
5. William Lloyd Garrison, *Selections From the Writings and Speeches of William Lloyd Garrison* (Boston: R.F. Wallcut, 1852), 95f.
6. ibid., 76-96.
7. Edwin H. Madden, *Civil Disobedience and Moral Law in the Nineteenth Century* (Seattle: University of Washington Press, 1968), 5.
8. Valarie H. Ziegler, *The Advocates of Peace in Antebellum America* (Bloomington, IN: Indiana University Press, 1992), 83.
9. In the 1865 edition of Francis Wayland, *The Elements of Moral Science* (Boston: Gould and Lincoln, 1865) he condemned war as in earlier editions but offered limited support to defensive war. "Force must be repelled by force, just as far as it is necessary to resist their evil design." 394.
10. Francis Wayland, *The Elements of Moral Science*, 4th ed. (Boston: Gould, Kendall, and Lincoln, 1840), 392.
11. ibid., 394.
12. ibid., 365.
13. ibid., 366f.
14. Francis Wayland, *University Sermons*, 3rd ed. (Boston, Gould, Kendall and Lincoln, 1850), 270.
15. *Millennial Harbinger*, 1846, 638-642.
16. Maddon, 33: Wayland, *The Elements of Moral Science*, (1865), 399.
17. ibid., 35.
18. *Christian Baptist*, I, 25.
19. *Millennial Harbinger*, (1832), 86.
20. ibid., 588f.
21. ibid., (1835), 587.
22. ibid., (1840), 99.
23. ibid., 102.
24. ibid., (1845), 235, 237.
25. ibid., 233f.
26. ibid., 240.
27. ibid., 195.
28. ibid., (1849), 413.

29. ibid., 251.
30. ibid., 278.
31. ibid., (1846), 6.
32. ibid., (1845), 109.
33. ibid., 239.
34. ibid., 240.
35. ibid., (1851), 27.
36. ibid., 202.
37. ibid., 27.
38. ibid., 29.
39. ibid., 624.
40. ibid., 247-249.
41. ibid., (1845), 240, emphasis mine.
42. ibid., (1851), 388.
43. ibid.
44. Earl Eugene Eminhizer, "Alexander Campbell's Thoughts on Slavery and Abolition," *West Virginia History*, 33/2 (Jan. 1972), 123.
45. ibid., 171f.
46. ibid., 53.
47. ibid., 224f.
48. Campbell, *Popular Lectures and Addresses*, 171.
49. *Millennial Harbinger*, (1845), 473.
50. Campbell, *Popular Lectures and Addresses*, 354.
51. ibid.
52. ibid.
53. ibid., 351.
54. ibid., 351-352.
55. ibid., 352.
56. ibid.
57. *Millennial Harbinger*, (1835), 587.
58. ibid., (1861), 348.

# Chapter 7

# Anti-War, Pro-Capital Punishment

All of Alexander Campbell's writings on war indicate that he was an absolute pacifist. He condemned wars of aggression and defensive wars alike. Repeatedly he insisted that Christians had no place in the military because the practice of war is utterly at odds with the spirit of Christianity. Further, Campbell taught that self-defense is contrary to the Christian life.[1] In all areas he stood for nonviolent solutions to human conflict. However, he made one exception. Campbell supported capital punishment as the penalty for the crime of murder. Such a position seems incompatible with his pacifism.

However, even Campbell himself recognized as much. In pointing out the consequences of abolishing capital punishment, he observed that if under no circumstances could one human have the right to take away the life of another there can be no right for nations to go to war. "I wonder not, then," he wrote, "that peace men are generally, if not universally, in favor of the total abolition of capital punishment for any crime whatever."[2]

## Peace Movement Dispute

In fact, peace advocates of the nineteenth century did not universally oppose capital punishment. During the time of Campbell's writing career there was a considerable amount of dispute among anti-war activists regarding the use of force in domestic affairs. Not all agreed that opposition to war entailed rejection of all forms of violence. Even among those who repudiated both aggressive and defensive wars were many who supported police action and the imposition of civil penalties, including capital punishment.

There had always been a considerable diversity of opinion among the members of the American Peace Society. As already observed, the organization included both absolute pacifists and those who maintained a qualified acceptance of defensive wars, those who viewed government as a servant of God for good, and those who considered it an instrument of evil and called Christians to withdraw from its workings. William Ladd, the first president of the American Peace Society, went through a considerable evolution in his own views of peace. Though he began by regarding defensive wars as morally permissible, eventually he came to condemn as evil all participation in war. But even after he became an absolute pacifist in regard to war, for a time he continued to support the use of the death penalty.[3] Many members of the American Peace Society shared his views.

Pertinent to this issue is an 1834 article Dr. William Allen, president of Bowdoin College and a vice-president of the American Peace Society, wrote as a rebuttal to Thomas Grimké. Entitled "Defensive War Vindicated," it was published in the *Calumet*, the Peace Society's journal. In the essay he argued that defensive wars were exercises in the enforcement of justice. The killing done by the defending army is not rightly classified as murder. Rather, he maintained such killing is more fairly viewed as similar to the execution of a murderer who has been convicted after due process of law.[4]

Grimké died before he finished writing his response to Allen. However, in 1835 the contents of the uncompleted manuscript appeared in the *Calumet*. Grimké spoke to the relationship between civil government and pacifism. He called into question Allen's assumption that the magistrate has a right to take human life. Grimké was firmly opposed to capital punishment in part because "the first duty of the Magistrate is the reformation of the offender."[5] This certainly could not be accomplished if the criminal is put to death.

Grimké contended that the activity of governing does not necessarily entail the use of deadly force. As a practicing lawyer, and a past state senator in South Carolina, he believed in the rule of law and held that the Christian citizen can make a meaningful contribution in government. But under no circumstances, Grimké argued, can the Christian support the taking of life. He acknowledged that the apostle Paul wrote that the governing authorities "beareth not the sword in vain" (Rom. 13:4). However, he saw in these words a metaphor for the broad right of government to punish criminals for breaking the law rather than as a justification of capital punishment. Further, he contended that a legitimate comparison cannot be made between the punitive function of civil government and fighting a defensive war since no world court or recognized international law was in existence.[6] Consequently, war is always a lawless activity. Alexander Campbell also made this point but to a very different end, as we will note.

The most thoughtful discussion of capital punishment and related issues in the nineteenth century came from a representative of the most extreme left wing of American pacifism, Adin Ballou, who was for a time president of the New England Non-Resistance Society. Ballou offered one of the most comprehensive philosophies of nonviolence found among nineteenth century pacifists. Ballou held that the primary cause of crime was poor social conditions. He chastised the wealthy for calling for harsh criminal penalties while doing little to help lift the poor from their misery. "Therefore, Christian non-resistance protests against the wickedness of the punishing as well as the punished classes," wrote Ballou.[7] He argued that the principle of retaliation and the practice of capital punishment was contrary to the spirit of Christian love which always focused on the redemption of the sinner. Several alternative means of dealing with the problem of crime and criminals were suggested by Ballou. However, he insisted, "The principle of non-injury must be inviolable ... What cannot be done uninjuriously must be left undone."[8]

Campbell's position on the relationship between pacifism and capital punishment is similar to that taken by the conservative peace advocate, the Rev. George Beckwith. As secretary of the American Peace Society in 1839, he wrote a response to the views of the Non-Resistance Society. While he advocated nonviolence in international affairs, he rejected the notion that human life must be inviolable in domestic affairs. He held that Jesus' teaching in the Sermon on the Mount regarding non-retaliating love applied to the relationship of individual to individual and to the relationship of nation to nation but was not applicable to the relationship of individual to nation. Because God had ordained government and bestowed on it the responsibility to punish those within a given society who act lawlessly, God had made an exception to the ethics of love.

Others had not been so forthright in admitting this apparent inconsistency. Beckwith wrote, "All penal acts are in direct, palpable contradiction of the precepts found in the Sermon on the Mount, and can be justified only on the ground of exception by the same authority that enjoined the former."[9] He did not embrace the abstract principle of the inviolability of human life, as did many peace activists. Rather he sought to be consistent with the Bible as he understood it by opposing war yet supporting capital punishment. Beckwith stated, "God permits the taking of life in one case, but not the other. He authorizes rulers to govern, but not to fight; to punish but not to quarrel. Such acts, even if they were physically the same, would be morally different."[10] Campbell agreed.

## Purpose of Punishment

Reformers in the 1840's – some of whom were peace activists – had succeeded in reducing, and in several states eliminating, the use of the death penalty. In many instances it was replaced with the penalty of imprisonment for life. Campbell was not pleased with this development. In September, 1845, he wrote in a short piece published in the *Millennial Harbinger* that he found this trend which "seems to be getting popular in the North... a troublesome one." He mentioned a particular murder case which caused him to "think there is especial force in the scriptural denunciation, 'Whoso sheddeth man's blood, by man shall his blood be shed.'"[11]

The following year Campbell returned to the topic in an essay he wrote for the Washington Literary Institute of Washington, Pennsylvania. The essay was entitled, "Is Capital Punishment Sanctioned by Divine Authority?" In it Campbell called into question the wisdom of those who would abolish capital punishment and he set forth his defense of the practice. He challenged what he believed was a misguided idea of the purpose of punishment held by the reformers of criminal law. To Campbell this issue touched the very "foundation of civil government."[12]

Campbell identified three purposes of punishment. These are the reformation of the criminal, protection of society and the satisfaction of justice. He was very critical of those of the "new school of philosophy [that] assume that the sole end of punishment is the reformation of the offender," and which advocates to re-educate the criminal so he or she can be reintegrated into society.[13] Campbell did not disagree that the reformation of criminals was important, but he maintained this was not the only legitimate concern. In the case of murderers reform was not a replacement for capital punishment. He held that, "strange though it may seem... the certainty of death is... the most efficient means of reformation."[14] Execution drove the murderer to see the need for repentance and a right relationship with God as nothing else could, thought Campbell.

However, Campbell believed the protection of society to be a more important reason for punishment. Life imprisonment was inadequate because there could be no iron-clad guarantee of protection for the innocent. Prisoners sometimes escaped. Governors may reprieve sentences. Murderers with influential connections may eventually be released. Campbell was concerned that without the death penalty the offender might murder again.[15] He believed that where capital punishment was not practiced, murder occurred more frequently. Capital punishment was seen by him as a deterrent to crime.

Finally, Campbell maintained that capital punishment was the only genuinely just punishment for a murderer. A life for a life was what he believed to be the biblical standard. The call for the abolishment of capital punishment most often arose from moral outrage over the death penalty being imposed on offenders for petty crimes, argued Campbell. Though before God all sin may be equally sinful, he held that not all crime is equally destructive to human society. He saw his own position as a moderate one. Campbell wrote, "Public opinion for more than a century has been vacillating between two extreme systems of punishment; one of which punishes more than a hundred varieties of offence with death, while the other inflicts death on no transgressor for any crime whatever."[16] Only murder was a crime worthy of the death penalty. Campbell favored changing the criminal code so that capital punishment would be the sentence for no lesser crime. He also supported making reforms in the criminal system to eliminate as much as possible the chance that an innocent person be executed. He firmly held "that an eye should not be taken for a tooth, nor a few years imprisonment for a man's whole life."[17] Campbell held that genuinely proportional retributive justice must be at work in the practice of capital punishment.

## Problems with Abolishing Capital Punishment

Early in his 1846 essay on capital punishment Campbell asks, "has man a right to take away the life of man on any account whatever?"[18] Though Campbell maintained that consideration of consequences should not determine one's position on moral issues, still he asked his audience to examine the "expediency" of abolishing capital punishment.[19] He pointed out three consequences of answering that question in the negative. Oddly, in light of what Campbell had written on war one might imagine he would find in the consequences he named reason to oppose the death sentence rather than to support it.

The first consequence of abolishing capital punishment was that the right to punish the criminal in any other form would be jeopardized as well. The reason for this was that any punishment could conceivably lead to the criminal's death. "A single strip may kill... How many die in jails, workhouses, penitentiaries, from causes to which they would not have been exposed but in those places of punishment!"[20] He made no mention of a need for more humane prison conditions, rather he argued for the importance of preserving the options of the authorities in punishing criminals.

The second consequence of abolishing the death penalty was that such an action would imply the end of war as a legitimate venture for nations. After all, wars are "originated and conducted on the assumption that man has a right, for just cause, to take away the life of man."[21] As previous chapters in this study have demonstrated, Campbell had made it plain from his earliest writings to his last that he wanted war abolished and believed no Christian should fight in any war. But in arguing for capital punishment he spoke of the end of war as an option for nations as though that would be an undesirable consequence. Clearly he was appealing to what he apparently believed were the values and concerns of his audience rather than expressing his own conviction in this matter. In fact he more clearly represented his own views in saying, "We may settle [national controversies] as we pacifically settle individual and corporate misunderstandings, and still argue against the abolition of capital punishment."[22]

Appealing to those who believe war is justifiable in some cases, Campbell wrote that "the fundamental fact must not be lost sight of – that nations can only do those things which every individual man had a right to do, anterior to the national form of society."[23] Strangely this is basically the same argument he used in his "Address on War" to make the opposite point. There he maintained that no one can do for the rights of the nation what one cannot do for one's own rights. Consequently, "unless a Christian man can go to war for himself, he cannot for the state."[24] Campbell held that Christians could not go to war for personal rights or self-defense, and, therefore, could not go to war for the state.

Given Campbell's anti-war views, this argument for capital punishment based on the right to go to war seems strikingly disingenuous.

The third of Campbell's supposedly undesirable consequences of claiming no one has a right to take the life of another in any circumstance is that to do so would imply a morally unfavorable view of heroes and patriots who have killed others.[25] In the denial of the right to kill another person there is an implicit judgment that much admired heroes who used deadly force were involved in morally dubious behavior. Again this argument seems not to reflect Campbell's own convictions in light of his writings both after and before his great 1846 defense of capital punishment. Two years later he wrote, "Forensic eloquence is full of the fame of great heroes, of military chieftains, of patriotic deliverers, whose memory must be kept forever verdant in the affections of a grateful posterity." But this he denounced as a "false spirit."[26] In 1830 Campbell contrasted the "boasting of their heroes" and the praises for "the bloody battles of the warrior," offered by "mere politicians of the land and the children of the flesh" to the "loftier song" and "purer joy" of Christians.[27] In defending capital punishment Campbell appears to make appeals to the supposed values of his audience that he not only did not share but had actually attacked on other occasions.

## Biblical Case for Capital Punishment

It is beyond the scope of this brief volume to look in detail at the biblical reasons behind Campbell's belief in capital punishment. An overview, however, is necessary. Largely he based his case on examples and laws in the Old Testament, which lend support to capital punishment. Campbell pointed to examples and statements, not just in the Jewish dispensation, but also in the Patriarchal age. A passage that had a key place in his argument reads, "Whoso sheddeth man's blood, by man shall his blood be shed: for in the image of God made he man." (Gen. 9:6)[28] Since the image of God in the human being is not limited to any period in history, Campbell argued, neither can capital punishment for murder be restricted to any age. "So long as it stands true that man was created in the image of God, so long it will bind every religious and moral people to take away the life of the murderer. It is, therefore, of immutable and perpetual obligation."[29]

Campbell maintained there is clear support for capital punishment in the New Testament, as well as the Old Testament. "It is sometimes assumed that the Messiah has forever abolished the bloody code of Moses and the patriarchs, and has preached more benevolence and forgiveness to the nations," he wrote, "What a baseless assumption!" Campbell conceded that Jesus did not come into the world to judge the world or be a civil lawgiver. As he did in his writings against war, Campbell referred to the not-of-this-world character of Christ's kingdom as Jesus spoke of it in his Sermon on the Mount. "In it he would not have an eye for an eye, tooth for tooth, or strip for strip."[30] Later that same year when writing on war Campbell declared, "This passage... ought to settle the war question forever."[31] He went on to scoff at those who claimed Jesus' words "only inhibited his servants from fighting for religion."[32]

But when Campbell turned his attention to capital punishment he did precisely what he chastised others for doing in relation to war – limiting the relevance of Jesus' words to the realm of religion. The fact that Jesus' kingdom was "not of this world" may have settled the war question for Campbell, but it certainly did not resolve the capital punishment issue. "[Jesus] would not have his followers to go to law for any violence, fraud, or wrong inflicted on them **on his account**... but for any wrong, violence, or compulsion inflicted on them **for their religion**... they were to endure it cheerfully."[33]

But Campbell resisted any broader application. Doing away with the practice of capital punishment apparently seemed to Campbell to be a step in the direction of anarchy. In fact, he virtually identifies opposition to the death penalty with opposition to government itself. "[H]e that hence argues for the abolition of civil government – of civil penalties – ... shocks all common sense."[34] It is possible that this statement is a rebuke to the more extreme pacifists such the members of the New England Non-Resistance Society. Campbell was convinced that civil government had the sanction of scripture and the coercion necessary to sustain human government was likewise approved by God. Though Campbell had argued that Jesus' command to Peter "to put up his sword into its place" essentially forbade Christians to "take up the sword" in defense of the nation from external threats, in dealing with internal criminal threats to the nation, Campbell chose to restrict the applicability of Jesus' words and instead commended the sword.[35]

But he was not without New Testament warrant. Citing the apostle Paul in Romans 13, Campbell noted that "the powers that be" are ordained of God and that the governing authorities are servants of God, "a messenger of wrath upon him that doeth evil." Campbell went on to say, "And, in the name of reason, why have a sword in the State, and worn by the civil magistrate, if it be unlawful or unchristian to put any one to death on any account whatever! It would, indeed, be to 'bear the sword in vain'; a thing which the Apostles themselves would have reprobated... The civil magistrate is now the civil avenger of blood."[36]

In contrast to Grimké, Campbell did not interpret these words metaphorically but accepted them as literal. Nor did Campbell contend that in "bearing the sword" the civil authorities were indirectly "servants of God", much as were the Babylonians or Assyrians who, according to the Bible, served God's purpose through not acting in a way approved for God's people. Rather he maintained that a Christian could actually execute a murderer. After all, "it is not the sword of the executioner. It is the hand of God – it is the sword of his justice that takes away that life which he himself gave."[37] This line of reasoning is not unlike that of John Calvin.[38] But it is directly at odds with his own repudiation of the idea that the Christian could bear the sword in war as a servant of God.

Finally, Campbell turned to the example of Jesus himself in defense of capital punishment. This does not appear to be a fruitful source from which to bolster a case for deadly force. Campbell admitted as much. The early ministry of Jesus was characterized by nonviolent love and the repudiation of violence. To this Campbell wrote, "While on earth he was a savior. In heaven he is now a king. Hereafter he will appear in the character of a judge and an avenger...We ask not what he did while on earth...But we ask, What did he when he became king, when exalted to be the prince and the governor of the universe?"[39]

Campbell did not focus his attention on Christ as one who will punish the impenitent. Rather his contention was that Christ threatened destruction on the wayward Jews of his time and carried out the threat within the context of history. "As governor of the world, he dispatched Titus with a Roman army, and laid siege to Jerusalem and to other cities in Judea. In the whole of these various wars and sieges – in the destruction of the city and the temple, he killed more than one million of them, and sent the remainder into exile." Campbell argued that as king of the nations, Christ continues to execute justice and punishment. "But he does it not in person, but by his ministers."[40]

In this defense of capital punishment, Campbell negates the earthly example of Christ in favor of the example of the exalted, royal Christ. The Prince of Peace gives way to the King of war. Further, Campbell ends up arguing for more than he intends. If his case does, indeed, successfully justify the death penalty, at the same time it sanctions war. Yet Campbell distinguished the killing done in war from the killing done with the implementation of the death penalty. He claimed only the latter is performed within a system of due process of law. War, on the other hand, is a lawless activity. This distinction does not hold if the example of Christ the King is appealed to as a warrant for human behavior. The destruction of Jerusalem was obviously not selective punishment of individuals for criminal behavior.

## Was Campbell Consistent?

Campbell freely cited the early church fathers as he built his case against war. However, he did not evoke them in his arguments for capital punishment. Among those he named in his "Address on War" was Tertullian. On the death penalty Tertullian wrote, "Even if he appeals to the power of the State, the servant of God should not pronounce capital sentences."[41] Such was the dominant position during the first three centuries of the church, just as pacifism was the prevailing position during this time in regard to war. The earliest Christians regarded all use of deadly force as incompatible with their faith. But Campbell had no interest in echoing their views. Rather, he cited them to undergird his own positions which rested on other grounds.

Campbell clearly believed there was no inconsistency in supporting capital punishment while opposing Christian participation in war. In his journal, the Millennial Harbinger, he did not hesitate to place side by side articles or interest pieces supporting capital punishment and others opposing participation in war.[42] From his perspective his consistency rested upon his fidelity to the teaching of scripture – and the New Testament in particular. The Bible, he believed, upheld capital punishment and forbade war.

But Campbell also saw a significant difference in the killing that occurred while carrying out a death penalty from the killing done during a mass conflict like a war. It was the difference between guilt and innocence. He wrote, "The right to take away the life of the murderer does not of itself warrant war, inasmuch as in that case none but the guilty suffer, whereas in war the innocent suffer not only with, but often without the guilty."[43] Capital punishment in America, Campbell believed, functioned within a context that upheld due process of law. Guilt had to be demonstrated before the death penalty could be imposed upon a person. War lacked a means of discrimination. In war, violence too often was inflicted on virtually anyone who happened to be in the way of the conflict.

But he opposed war not only because he was concerned about the inadvertent deaths of non-combatants. He was equally concerned for the innocent soldiers. Campbell viewed war as a conflict started by the guilty and fought by the innocent. He wrote that "the most convincing argument against a Christian becoming a soldier may be drawn from the fact that he fights against an innocent person – I say innocent person, so far as the cause of war is contemplated."[44] Soldiers too often fight for reasons they do not truly understand, against men they do not know and at the command of leaders of questionable motive. In contrast to war, capital punishment as a penalty for murder does not lead to indiscriminate killing. For Campbell that difference enabled him to support the practice.

It has been suggested that perhaps the circumstances of the early to mid-nineteenth century America played a role in shaping these issues for Campbell. During this period the United States did not face any major external threat. Yet murder remained a problem within the nation.[45] Such historical circumstances cannot be entirely discounted as an influence in Campbell's thought. Still it appears biblical and theological considerations were the primary factors shaping his position.

Of the two issues, capital punishment and opposition to war, the issue that captured Campbell's attention more deeply and enduringly was clearly war. His pacifism was evident throughout his career as dozens of entries in The Christian Baptist and the Millennial Harbinger testify. In contrast, Campbell addressed capital punishment on relatively few occasions within a fairly narrow span of years. Nevertheless, his views in this matter cannot be discounted nor easily harmonized with his advocacy for nonviolence. His support of capital punishment remains a conspicuous exception to Campbell's otherwise thoroughgoing pacifism.

## Notes

1. *Millennial Harbinger*, (1848), 372.
2. *Millennial Harbinger*, (1846), 126.
3. Valarie H. Ziegler, *The Advocates of Peace in Antebellum America* (Bloomington, IN: Indiana University Press, 1992), 55.
4. Peter Brock, *Radical Pacifists in Antebellum America* (Princeton: Princeton University Press, 1968), 57.
5. ibid., 59.
6. ibid.
7. Brock, 156.
8. ibid., 157.
9. quoted in Ziegler, 84.
10. quoted in Brock, 175.
11. *Millennial Harbinger*, (1845), 424.
12. ibid., (1846), 124.
13. ibid., 127.
14. ibid., 128.
15. ibid.
16. ibid., 130.
17. ibid., 131.
18. ibid., 125.
19. ibid.
20. ibid.
21. ibid.
22. ibid., 126.
23. ibid., 125.
24. *Millennial Harbinger*, (1848), 372.
25. *Millennial Harbinger*, (1846), 126f.
26. *Millennial Harbinger*, (1848), 380.
27. ibid., 377, 378.
28. *Millennial Harbinger*, (1846), 136.
29. ibid., 138.

30. ibid., 142.
31. ibid., 639.
32. ibid., 640.
33. ibid., 142, 143.
34. ibid., 143.
35. ibid., 641; also *Millennial Harbinger*, (1848), 375.
36. ibid., 143.
37. ibid., 145.
38. John Calvin, *Institutes of the Christian Religion 2*, trans. Ford Lewis Battles (Philadelphia: Westminster Press, 1960), 1497ff.
39. *Millennial Harbinger*, (1846), 146.
40. ibid.
41. cited in Francesco Compagnoni, "Capital Punishment and Torture in the Tradition of the Roman Catholic Church," in *The Death Penalty and Torture*, ed. by Franz Bockle and Jacques Pohier (New York: Crossroad/Seabury, 1979), 46.
42. *Millennial Harbinger*, (1846), 706.
43. *Millennial Harbinger*, (1848), 383.
44. ibid., 377.
45. Lunger, *The Political Ethics of Alexander Campbell*, (St. Louise: Bethany Press, 1954), 242, 262.

# Chapter 8

# A Future For A Pacifist Past?

"All attempts to interpret the past are indirect attempts to understand the present and its future," wrote H. Richard Niebuhr.[1] How true. The past is not merely an artifact to be examined as an end in itself, but an instrument to be used as we seek to think and live more faithfully now and in years to come. In examining the thought of Alexander Campbell on pacifism and war, what do we find that will contribute to our endeavor to be people of God's peace in the midst of the violence of our own time? Surely we cannot simply echo Campbell's teaching without reassessment and revision. On the other hand, it will not be most productive to merely criticize the shortcomings of his ideas and altogether discard them. So in this final chapter, I will indicate some aspects of Campbell's thought that I think are most fruitful – and also point out ways in which his thinking is not altogether adequate – as we seek to understand and practice the peaceable way of Jesus Christ today.

## Centrality of Jesus Christ and Cross-Bearing Discipleship

Nothing was more central to Campbell's opposition to war and violence than the example and words of Jesus Christ. Only Jesus could issue a divine warrant for Christians to be involved in warfare. Not only had he never given such a warrant, his own life and teachings pointed to a way of being in the world that eliminates war as a possibility. Campbell urged Christians not to "forget the victories of Him who did not lift up his voice in the streets" but instead to imitate Jesus' "spirit of mildness, meekness and unostentatious heroism." He contrasted the example left by Jesus with that of the war hero, and he urged Christians to refrain from extolling "the bloody battles of the warrior."[2] Jesus did, indeed, engage in war but his weapon was the Word of God, the sword of the Spirit. His was a nonviolent mode of warfare through which he sought to conquer by love. His aim was not to destroy enemies but to transform them, replacing hostility with reconciliation.

Campbell rightly recognized that the love taught and embodied by Jesus Christ subverted the narrower love of family, nation or race. The more confined type of love, he argued, often "conceals self-interest under the mask of public spirit."[3] In contrast, the love to which Christians are called extends beyond the barriers and boundaries that normally constrain people. It is a love that is universal in its nature. It is not a love that can inspire violence on behalf of the one against the other, deeming one worthy of protection and the other deserving of destruction. A love that is reflective of Jesus Christ and worthy to be called Christian "embraces all Christians in its affection, and all mankind in its benevolence."[4]

While Campbell frequently stressed the nonviolent love taught and, indeed, commanded by Christ, he understood the importance of the demonstration of this love in the life of Christ. Love cannot finally be demanded and compelled by force. It must be won. Thus, Christ came as the demonstration of God's love that evokes love as a response. "To fill men with love to him, he shows them that he loves them. They say, 'we love him because he first loved us,'"[5] wrote Campbell. God in Christ is not only the wellspring of love but the definition of love. Citing Soame Jenyns, Campbell contrasted a patriotic love that allowed room for violence against enemies, with the love shown by God for all humankind. He concludes, "Christianity enjoins us to imitate the universal benevolence of our Creator, who pours forth his blessings on every nation upon earth."[6]

The call to imitate God in love is profoundly biblical. Never is there a mandate in the New Testament to imitate God in power, wrath or vengeance. But repeatedly calls are issued to emulate God in acts of compassion, forgiveness, suffering and service. The following passages are just a few of many found in the New Testament that point to the sort of imitation that is intrinsic to discipleship.

> "But I say to you, love your enemies…so that you may be children of your Father in heaven; for he makes his sun rise on the evil and on the good…"(Matthew 5: 44 – 45).

"But love your enemies... Your reward will be great, and you will be children of the Most High; for he is kind to the ungrateful and the wicked. Be merciful, just as your Father is merciful" (Luke 6: 35 – 36).

"So as I, Your Lord and Teacher, have washed your feet, you also ought to wash one another's feet. For I have set you an example, that you should do as I have done to you" (John 13: 14 – 15).

"I give you a new commandment, that you should love one another. Just as I have loved you, you should also love one another" (John 13: 34).

"This is my commandment that you love one another as I have loved you. No one has greater love than this, to lay down his life for one's friend" (John 15: 12 – 13).

"Bear with one another and, if anyone has a complaint against another, forgive each other; just as the Lord has forgiven you, so you must also forgive" (Colossians 3: 13).

"And be kind to one another, tenderhearted, forgiving one another, as God in Christ has forgiven you" (Ephesians 4: 32).

"If you endure when you are beaten for doing wrong, what credit is that? But if you endure when you do right and suffer for it, you have God's approval. For to this you have been called, because Christ also suffered for you, leaving you an example, so that you should follow in his steps" (1 Peter 2: 20 – 21).

"By this we may be sure that we are in him: whoever says, 'I abide in him,' ought to walk just as Christ walked" (1 John 2: 5 – 6).

Campbell pointed to the need to imitate God in love and to follow the example of Jesus, though, perhaps, he did not do so with the emphasis and clarity that is called for in our own time. Still he lifted up Jesus' command to love enemies, bless those who curse you and do good to those who hate you, noting that this startling teaching was not just conveyed by Jesus' words but also "enforced by his example."[7]

To follow Jesus is not to imitate the cultural peculiarities of a particular first century Palestinian man: his dress, diet, profession, mode of transportation or language. Rather it is to be like him as he manifests certain aspects of the character of God and thus requires that we pay attention to how he lived in relation to others. He did not display God's judgment and capacity for vengeance. Rather in his life self-giving service, truthful speech and non-violent love were embodied. Not self-assertion and the compulsion to control, but self-renunciation characterized the life of Jesus.

To follow Jesus is to imitate his practice of self-giving love. It is to relinquish the often violent quest for control and instead accept faith-filled vulnerability. In saying, "If any would come after me let them deny themselves and take up their cross and follow me" (Mark 8: 34), Jesus called for disciples to follow him in a life of far-reaching sacrificial service which is not limited by even self-preservation (Mark 10: 45). Rather such a life is shaped by the one who goes to the cross.

While Jesus rejected the violent power of coercion, his life certainly was powerful. But his was not the power to compel. Rather it was a power from God that comes from giving up all but the desire to be in the service of God. This is the power of truth which stands against the power to force others to comply to aims imposed on them. Jesus challenged those around him and confronted those in authority so that people who heard him were amazed at the exceptional authority of his words (Matthew 7: 28 – 29). Yet he did not force others to submit to him. His power left room for the sort of vulnerability that made it possible for Jesus to be taken by human hands and be nailed to a cross as a victim of those who refused to embrace his lordship.

The example of Jesus that is deserving of imitation is found precisely in his manner of loving and supremely as that love was shown in the cross. It is at this very point that the place of Christ is weakest in the pacifism of Alexander Campbell. The teachings of Christ are prominent, the example of Christ is present but the cross of Christ is largely missing as Campbell calls Christians to live in peace, which is a significant failing in his thinking.

The cross stands nearby whenever there is a biblical call to imitate God in Christ.[8] "The story of the cross...is first of all a story of how God treats enemies. Those who come to know the love of God in Christ have experienced the love of One who has responded to enemies, not with vengeance or violence, but with unmerited love," Michael Gorman has observed. "To have faith in this God is thus to be embraced by such love; to pass it on to others is the only proof of having received it."[9] It is not love by any definition that counts as Christian but love shaped by the cross. Christian pacifism cannot be adequately Christ-centered if it is not cross-centered. The cross is the measure of faith, hope, love, service, power and everything that we call "spirituality."

The cross provides the lens through which we see the world and provides the form by which we are to live in it. It is for this reason that claims made from the time of Augustine to our own that Christian soldiers can kill in war and yet practice love even in that very act are not credible. Surely it is possible to kill and destroy without hate; training can develop that capacity. But if love is defined by the cross, there is no room for making victims and creating misery either in one's personal life or for the sake of a nation–state. Love reflective of the cross endures suffering rather than inflicting it and accepts death rather than causing it. Christ-centered love is cross-centered and for that reason it is non-violent in all of its ways.

Campbell's support of capital punishment was possible only because he failed to be cross-centered in his pacifism. His attempt to justify Christian support of capital punishment by enlisting the exalted Christ who acts now as sovereign over history and will come as judge and avenger is deeply flawed. The appeal to the exalted Christ is totally out of keeping with the pattern of ethical admonition found in the New Testament. It is precisely in the relinquishment of power that Christ and God are models of behavior for Christians. The power of God to punish, coerce and control is not seen as ethically relevant by the authors of the New Testament. To the contrary, it is because of God's role as avenger that Christians were expressly forbidden to take revenge. Instead they were commanded to bless and not curse those who subjected them to persecution and to feed and give drink to enemies, not repaying evil with evil but overcoming evil with good (Romans 12: 14 – 21).

It is not likely that Paul sought to take the sword of vengeance from the hands of Christians in Romans 12 just to put it back into their hands, as Campbell suggested the apostle did, in the following chapter of the epistle. The sword is placed by God in the hands of the state, not in the hands of the church, according to Paul. Christians are not addressed as agents of the state in Romans 13: 1–7 but as subjects of the state. Here Christians are not instructed as to their function on behalf of the state. Rather Paul informs them of the state's function on behalf of God. While Christians are to "repay no one evil for evil" (Romans 12: 17), the state does this very thing. It acts as "a terror" to bad conduct (Romans 13: 3). The governing authority is "the servant of God to execute his wrath on the wrongdoer" (13: 4). It is the non-Christian state, not Christians as functionaries of the state, that "bear the sword." Christians are called upon to recognize the God-ordained role of the state and "be subject." Being "subject" does not include killing at the bidding of the state, either in war or domestically to preserve social order and safety. The notion that Romans 12: 14 – 21 addresses Christians "as individuals" while Romans 13: 1 – 7 is guidance for Christian as participating citizens and functionaries of the state, as Campbell uses the passage, is without foundation within the text. In every circumstance the calling of the Christian is one and the same: "Owe no one anything, except to love one another... Love does no wrong to a neighbor; therefore love is the fulfilling of the law" (Romans 13: 8, 10). This calling is kept in focus when pacifism is cross-centered.

There is no way to follow Jesus that is not marked by the cross, which means that being a disciple of Christ entails living in a way that leaves one vulnerable to abuse and even death. Following him in truthfulness and servanthood cannot be done without also following him in defenselessness, for that is the nature of the truth and service he offered. In his compassionate healings and penetrating teaching Jesus displayed the power of God. But he also displayed the self-chosen powerlessness of God in his crucifixion. The lives of those who follow Jesus bear witness to his non-retaliatory, self-sacrificing way. Hence, Paul could say, "While we live, we are always being given up to death for Jesus' sake, so that the life of Jesus may also be visible in our mortal flesh" (2 Corinthians 4: 11).

This certainly does not suggest that people must endure violence they can avoid or escape. Even Jesus evaded a hostile crowd in Nazareth (Luke 4:

29 – 30). The cross does not encourage the abandonment of all resistance to abuse or oppression. Nor does it simply endorse victimization. The way of the cross is a way that is chosen, not imposed by other people. There are means of nonviolent resistance that have been effective in opposing victimization and oppression. Surely they are not always effective, but the same can be said of violence and war. Still, effectiveness, while desirable, is not to supersede the way of the cross. As Luke Timothy Johnson has written, "The imitation of Christ in his life of suffering and service – not as an act of masochism for the sake of suppressing one's own life but as an act of love for the enhancement of other's life – is not an optional version of Christian identity. It is the very essence of Christian identity."[10] The cross is not an emblem of victimization so much as an eloquent demonstration of love by One who willingly took his place with victims to save both them and their oppressors. The cross is not just the means of salvation but the shape of Christian existence. To affirm one without the other is to be left with a fragmented, incomplete faith.

Insisting, not just on Christ-centeredness, but cross-centeredness both places pacifism on more solidly biblical ground and disarms those who contend pacifism is foolishly unrealistic and naïve. When all the concentration is placed upon the teachings of Jesus, apart from his death, pacifism can be taken to be a simplistic strategy for achieving harmony in the world. If pacifism is a strategy, then it is like war insofar as its aim is to achieve desirable outcomes in worldly affairs. Its value is demonstrated in its capacity to deliver certain consequences: freedom, justice, democracy or some other chosen goal. "Love your enemies" then is seen as a means of changing the enemy who some may imagine will be impelled to love in return and respond to kindness with kindness. Of course sometimes this may occur; sometimes not.

However, a pacifism that is cross-centered is not first of all a strategy to end war. The measure of its truthfulness is not found in its success in bringing about pleasing consequences on the stage of history. While there certainly is a place for the consideration of consequences in Christian ethics, that place is not front and center. Rather, pacifism arises from the call to be like Jesus regardless of the consequences. The cross displays the outcome of the nonviolently loving life lived by Jesus and those who walk in his steps. He repeatedly taught his disciples not to expect any better treatment for themselves than he would receive. There is nothing naïve or unrealistic to be found in this pacifism. The

Christ-centered nonviolent life of love bears witness to God's way in Christ. It is a life lived in the conviction that God more desires to use our vulnerable faithfulness than our most clever calculation of consequences, and that God will make history come out right without our violent maneuvers.

## Church Unity and Nonviolence

For Campbell pacifism was never merely an issue for the individual Christian. Rather he recognized that the nature of the church itself demands nonviolence. The church in one place is bound to and owes loyalty to the church in every other place. National allegiance – as well as other matters such as racial identity, or class interest or cultural background – must not be allowed to override Christian unity. Campbell wrote, "The true Christian church, or house of God, is composed of all those in every place that do publicly acknowledge Jesus of Nazareth as the true Messiah, and the only Savior of men; and, building themselves upon the foundation of the Apostles and Prophets, associate under the constitution which he himself has granted and authorized in the New Testament, and are walking in his ordinances and commandments – and of none else."[11] He went on to say that the church is a "community of communities" built on the same foundation regardless of where it might be located. Though local manifestations of the church manage their own particular affairs as their unique situations demand, nevertheless they are "by virtue of one common Lord, one faith, one baptism and one common salvation, but one kingdom or church of God, and, as such, are under obligations to cooperate with one another in all measures promotive of the great ends of Christ's death and resurrection… to the ends of the earth."[12]

As noted in the second chapter of this study, Campbell – from his earliest writings onward – condemned the willingness of Christians throughout the world to align themselves with their respective nations and fight against one another in war. He understood that few behaviors could be more detrimental to the practice of church unity and the promotion of the gospel of peace than Christians participating in warfare. While violence against anyone is contrary to both the teachings and example of Jesus Christ, violence of Christians upon one another is an attack upon the work of the Holy Spirit. "For by one Spirit we were all baptized into one body – Jews or Greeks, slaves or free – and all were made to drink of one Spirit" (1 Corinthians 12: 13). Christians fighting on opposing sides against each other in war suggests that the church is actually at war against itself. In Campbell's view, to see war as simply a conflict between nations is not to see it truthfully. So long as Christians are involved in the conflict the rightful reign of Christ is distorted and misrepresented before the watching world. The reign, the rule, the kingdom of Christ is one. Under the Lordship of Jesus Christ the church cannot set itself against itself for the sake of mutually hostile nations without betraying the Lord and undermining the identity and mission of the church. No cause, including the defense of the innocent – always understood in a most partisan manner during war – is superior to the cause of the church.

For the Christian and the church, national survival cannot be an absolute end. The integrity of the church and its witness transcends national interests and even national survival. Insofar as the churches throughout the world fail to repudiate the Christian participation in warfare, oneness in Christ will be treated as dispensable and subject to the Christians' loyalty to the separated and often hostile nations. Only a nonviolent church can be united sufficiently to witness to Jesus as Lord that the world might believe.

The church exists, not to help preserve present institutions, but to be a precursor of the kingdom of God. A church divided along lines of nation, race or class speaks not of a promised future but of a sinful and hostile present. If the church does not repudiate the violence that too often accompanies division between competing bodies in the world, the church will likely be reduced to allowing others to set the boundaries of its service and love. The church will be incapable of showing the world anything it does not already see.

Campbell's emphasis upon the unity of the church as a reason to repudiate war is among the most distinctive and important contributions he makes to a Christian pacifism. He points out that regardless of where the church is found it does not truly belong in that place. Rather, all the congregations and all the Christians who are members of those congregations exist as "'strangers,' or aliens, in these respective nations." Yet they are "collectively 'a holy nation – a royal priesthood – a particular people.'"[13] The true identity of both church and the Christian is not based upon nationality but is given by God in Christ. For this reason the attachment and loyalty of Christians to one another – regardless of where they might live – is more significant than that attachment and loyalty which comes from earthly citizenship. Each and every Christian is part of one family of faith, and, as Campbell pointed out, "a Christian is not born where he lives; he is born from above... Is not the bond of union... faith or the new birth?"[14]

National unity and global Christian unity are not likely to harmoniously coexist. These are competing, not compatible, versions of unity.[15] National interest cannot be given priority by a people who take seriously the admonition to "do good to all, *and especially* to those of the household of faith" (Galatians 6: 10). Only as the church detaches itself from the narrow unity rooted in and fostered by the nation-state will it be able to develop a faithful global imagination and act in view of it to minister to the world as it ought. When the church in the United States – or any other nation – compliantly helps reinforce national unity, inevitably this compliance will weaken the credibility of the church's witness to the God who loves the entire world. Concern for national unity tends to be most acute precisely when there is a perceived external threat. The church within the nation is expected by those in power to cooperate with the effort to resist the threat. Yet the ministry of reconciliation and the support of one nation's animosity against another nation cannot walk hand-in-hand without the church's identity and its ministry of reconciliation becoming grossly disfigured into something that cannot be legitimately recognized as Christian. This is destructive both to the unity of the church and the unity of the world. Only a unity that rests upon the revelation of God in Christ is adequate to who we are as Christians and as humans.

To the extent that the church willingly shares in the divisions of the world, reflecting them in its own life, it has betrayed the one Lord. The church does not exist to bolster any of the pieces of the fragmented world against any other, but to offer an alternative to them. The church exists to show the world that its brokenness is not necessary. Christ has come into the world to make peace, breaking down the wall of hostility to create one new people (Ephesians 2: 11 – 22). Jesus Christ is the one cornerstone upon which the church must be built. The church cannot rest its identity or practice on anything else. Rather the church is to show in its life that the hurtful divisions of the world are neither inevitable nor unbreachable. To do this Christians must see themselves as a people of peace who live in every place and with every race as strangers and sojourners. Home for Christians is the church, not the nation.[16]

As the church is one by its nature, according to Campbell, so too this oneness is made apparent in the worship of the church. Campbell deplored the practice of Christians debarring each other from the Lord's Table "because of doctrinal or political differences."[17] He maintained, "All Christians are members of the house or family of God, are called and constituted a holy and royal priesthood, and may, therefore, bless God for the Lord's table, its loaf, and cup – approach it without fear, and partake of it with joy as often as they please, in remembrance of the death of their Lord and Saviour."[18] Campbell was perfectly clear in his insistence that those who were welcome and united at the one table are not are of a single region or nation, but rather are a unique and far-flung people formed by God.[19]

At the Lord's Table it is as though Christ says to every disciple, "For you my body was wounded; for you my life was taken." In receiving the bread and cup the disciple says, according to Campbell, "Lord, I believe it. My life springs from thy suffering; my joy from thy sorrows; and my hope of glory everlasting from thy humiliation and abasement even to death." Campbell recognized the Lord's Supper, not just as a sacred occasion for the individual believers to attach themselves to Christ like separate spokes connected to the hub of a wheel. Rather he saw that in the Lord's Supper believers are to turn to one another and celebrate the God-blessed tie that binds them together. He writes, "Each disciple, in handing the symbols to his fellow disciple, says, in effect, 'You, my brother, once an alien, are now a citizen of heaven; once a stranger, are now brought home to the family of God. You have owned my Lord as your Lord, my people as your people. Under Jesus the Messiah we are one.'" At the Lord's Supper the Christian "knows no man after the flesh," rather "[t]ies that spring from eternal love" are what most deeply matter.[20] All natural connections and earth-bound unities are transcended in the bread and cup of communion.

While Campbell does not expressly pursue the implications of the practice of the Lord's Supper for a war-torn world, his teachings are filled with subversive potential. Any participation in communion that is attentive and faithful to the truths to which the Lord's Supper points will undermine whatever attachment, unity or loyalty there is that could set Christian against Christian in war. Though the Lord's Supper is always celebrated in a specific location, participation in the sacred meal unites Christians in each place with those in every other place. By faith the local is always linked to the universal. When the reality of faith takes effect, distinctions among Americans, Iraqis, Russians, Cubans and Chinese are abolished as truly as were the distinctions between Jew and Greek, barbarian and Scythian (Colossians 3: 10) in the first century. In the practice of the Lord's Supper, our eyes are opened to the truth of God in Christ and the truth of being the body of Christ. On the other hand, eating and drinking "without discerning the body" (1 Corinthians 11: 29) allows the detrimental divisions and distinctions of the world to intrude into the practice of being church. The Lord's Supper ceases to genuinely be the Lord's Supper at all but is reduced to a ritual that serves the self-interests of an unfaithful church that has been conformed to the deformity of the world. When participated in with integrity, the Lord's Supper "transgresses national boundaries and redefines who our fellow-citizens are... The eschatological breakdown of divisions between Jew and Greek – and all other natural and social divisions – is preeminently made present in the Eucharistic feast," as William Cavanaugh observes.[21] Only by learning to worship in a disciplined and attentive way can the church resist the corrosive effects of national unity and identity enough to truly be itself.

At the Lord's Table the church retells and remembers the story of its crucified Lord and Savior. The church learns anew the kind of love that brought it into being and in turn the kind of love members are to share with one another and the world. At the Table, the church receives the blessings purchased by the sacrificial love of God and is called to respond by practicing forgiveness, offering hospitality and embodying peace. In eating the bread and drinking of the cup of communion, the church is placed with the One who relinquished coercive power and absorbed violence without reprisal or revenge. In attentively celebrating the Lord's Supper, the church learns how to be the people God called it to be.

## Anti-war Strategy and War in the Particular

Campbell's pacifism, however, has been criticized for failing to deal with the church's relation to war in the concrete and for "turning from a discussion of the particular war to a discussion of war in general."[22] This criticism is certainly justified, but whether this is a shortcoming or not is a matter for discussion. The need to analyze the specific details of a particular war are not as crucial for a pacifist as for one in the just war tradition, at least insofar as the decision to oppose the war is concerned. For one working within the just war tradition the decision whether or not to support or oppose a particular war hinges upon whether certain criterion are or are not met by one's nation. For a pacifist like Campbell it is not the peculiar characteristics of war at a certain time and place that may demand Christian opposition, but the abiding character of discipleship that demands it. Attending to the unique elements of particular wars would have contributed little to Campbell's antiwar position. What he found in war that was abhorrent and contrary to Christian existence was and is present in all wars.

Further, the central strategy he advocated in opposition to war was the same for every war: Christian non-participation. While Campbell was clearly supportive of the state as a divinely ordained institution and he advocated almost unquestioningly obedience to the governing authorities, he called for unflinching resistance when it came to war. As it has been made clear in the preceding chapters of this study, he saw no place for the Christian in the military. The choice to oppose war and refuse to participate or to lend support to a war effort was a choice of light against darkness in Campbell's view. Apparently he believed Christians could lead the nations toward a repudiation of war if Christians would set the example by refusing to use deadly force in international conflicts.

So long as Christians were willing to add their efforts to the hostilities between nations, any other supposedly Christian strategy to end war would lack credibility. Of course Campbell did not view non-participation in war primarily in terms of a strategy to pressure nations to behave in certain more peaceable ways. Pacifism was above all an expression of obedience to Christ regardless of its strategic effectiveness, as has already been noted. Still, he believed that living in conformity to the nonviolent, loving ways of Christ would have an impact on the nations. Consequently, convincing Christians to reject war was his first concern, both for the sake of the fidelity of the church and for the sake of the well-being of the world.

This emphasis is one that needs to be recaptured in our time, I believe. Peace advocacy that is aimed at dissuading a war-ward direction in national policy – while commendable – is not the primary concern of the church. Fostering faithfulness is. Careful and persistent education that shows the incompatibility of violence with the example of Jesus and the teachings of the New Testament is imperative. The development of congregations capable of supporting and nurturing nonconformity to socially sanctioned uses of deadly force is a crucial task. A willingness to openly discourage Christians from entering the military is much needed. Promoting deeper loyalty and fellowship among Christians of various nations is critical. Such actions are necessary if the church is to be a credible agent of God's peace and a model of God's will for the world.

While the church was his first concern, Campbell certainly did not suggest that Christian peace advocacy should not extend beyond simple non-participation. He wrote, "We have all much interest in the question [of war]; we can all do something about it, and it is everyone's duty to do all the good he can. We must create a public opinion on this subject. We should inspire a pacific spirit, and show off on all proper occasions the chief objections to war."[23] Clearly Campbell wanted nonviolence taught and war opposed in as many venues as possible. He urged that alternative means of settling disputes be devised and implemented.

Still, his own programmatic agenda was sparse. However, he was a supporter of a World Congress. This proposal was a centerpiece in the literature of the American Peace Society and was promoted by its first president, William Ladd, throughout his life. Campbell adopted the proposal, calling for a "by-law-established umpire" which would serve as a "High Court of Nations for adjudicating and terminating all international misunderstandings and complaints, redressing and remedying all wrongs and grievances."[24] Without national sovereignty being relinquished to some degree by all nations and submission to binding arbitration by an international institution of justice, Campbell believed war would continue to be inevitable and the resolution of disputes that followed wars would be unjust. Thus, he suggested that nations devise a more rational and humane approach to international problem-solving and thereby outlaw war.

One can only speculate about the degree to which he would be supportive of international ventures such as the United Nations or the World Court. Evidence from Campbell's writings suggests that he would likely be sympathetic to their work, given his call for an international conflict resolution organization. Still while he did not eschew concrete strategies for international peacemaking, he placed his emphasis elsewhere. Instead he focused his energy on laying out biblical, theological and humanitarian reasons for adopting nonviolence and pragmatic reasons for deploring war.

While strategic efforts and theological thinking about peace are not necessarily at odds, sometimes concrete strategies become disconnected from theological underpinnings. Speaking from years of experience of working with Christian peace groups, I've found that in some circles Christian peace activists are far clearer about their commitment to chosen secular strategies than they are to theological and biblical foundations for their aims. Peace and justice ministries in mainline churches have been criticized – sometimes by sympathetic insiders – for too often going about their work in a manner that is little different from secular institutions that work toward peace and justice. That criticism is not without foundation.[25]

If it is a shortcoming in Campbell's writings that he opposed war in general but did not sufficiently deal with concrete means of opposing specific wars, this is a shortcoming to be preferred to allowing the biblical and theological considerations of the church to play a secondary role and exhibiting a preoccupation with influencing the state. Concern for incarnating the peaceable way of Christ in the life of the church for the sake of the world must not be underplayed as an obvious priority while the focus is placed on attempts to alter the war-prone policies of the state. To do so undermines Christian pacifism. Remarking on the abandonment of pacifism on the part of some Christians in the aftermath of the terrorist attacks of September 11, 2001, Patrick Nugent, director of the Center of Quaker Thought and Practice at Earlham College, observed, "Pacifists whose convictions are the fruit of secular strategic reasoning tend to collapse when confronted with the strategic weaknesses of pacifism ...[P]acifism... at its best is a response of discipleship..."[26] Concrete strategies for opposing specific wars are important but not more important than offering clear and compelling reasons for being a peaceable people of God whether certain nonviolent methods for reducing deadly conflict and war are effective or not.

This is not to suggest that war in general should be opposed but opposition to a war in particular ought to be muted. Neither is this to suggest that pacific faithfulness is all that matters and considerations of strategic effectiveness when opposing war and violence are irrelevant. Faithfulness is not in simple opposition to the quest for effectiveness. In fact, Christians can remain steadfast in their efforts in the eschatological conviction that in the long run faithfulness and effectiveness are in complete harmony. In the short run, nonviolent strategies to resist war and violence do not always work, something that can be said of violent means to attain goals as well as observed earlier. While the church seeks to be effective, the church must be concerned not only with what its actions accomplish but also with what its actions say. If the church's actions fail to declare God's self-sacrificing, nonviolent love, then regardless of what is concretely accomplished in the short run; in the long run the church fails not only God but the world as well.[27]

## Resurrection, the Kingdom of God, and the Future

The church is not just God's people of the present but a sign of the future. For Campbell the church is the "one Kingdom of Christ in the world" over which Jesus is sovereign.[28] Campbell often referred to the church as "the Kingdom of Heaven," not because the church ***is*** heaven but because it ***pertains*** to heaven, with hope, blessings, privileges and laws – the supreme law being love – that are "not of this world."[29] What the church is in the present points to the future that is coming. "The whole earth is the present territory of the Kingdom of Heaven, but the new heaven and earth are to be its inheritance," wrote Campbell.[30] The church lives among the nations but "seeks a better country," a "city yet to come." For Campbell, then, the church is an eschatological community, longing for, pointing to and proleptically embodying the future God has promised.

Campbell's understanding of the church is intimately connected to his ideas about the millennium. As noted earlier, Campbell believed a united, restored church was necessary to usher in the millennium. He rejected the notion that the return of Christ would be a sudden and cataclysmic response to a world in deepening corruption and rebellion toward God. To the contrary, Campbell believed God is at work in the world – particularly through the ministry and mission of the church – to evangelize and to serve in ways that will positively influence the world. He saw the world for the most part on a path of improvement and believed this to be evidence of a sovereign God at work.

It was his conviction that Christians should cooperate with God by fostering social advancements and reforms, always with an eye to the millennium, that "state of greatly enlarged and continuous prosperity, in which the Lord will be exalted and his divine spirit enjoyed in unprecedented measure."[31] While he did not claim that human efforts can actually bring about the millennium, he did believe the church and its members should prepare for it by promoting conditions that are fitting for the millennial age and, beyond that, to when Christ returns and the "structure of the earth is changed – new heavens and earth occupy its place – and instead of being with the Lord a thousand years on this earth, his people will be with him in a new earth to all eternity."[32]

The particulars of Campbell's eschatology need not be embraced in order for us to recognize the importance of eschatology for the life of the church and the practice of peace. Certainly, one need not agree with Campbell's virtual identification of the church with the kingdom of Christ to see the church as the sign and foretaste of the reign of God. The church can be understood in such a way because the kingdom or reign of God was embodied in Jesus Christ, the head of the church. Campbell's millennial hope fostered in him a peaceable imagination enabling him to see an alternative reality. This dimension of his pacifist thought has much to commend it. In no way does it depend upon the peculiarities of post-millennialism.

Jesus came preaching the kingdom of God. He declared the presence of the future. "The kingdom of God is at hand," he proclaimed. In his parables, through his healings and wonders, by means of his association with disreputable outsiders, in his words of forgiveness and his nonviolent love, Jesus displayed the kingdom of God in his own person. In everything the rule and reign of God filled his life. The presence of the kingdom of God in Jesus Christ was such that the world could not continue unchanged. Hence, the announcement and presence of God in Christ was coupled with the call, "Repent!" In light of God's future made present in Jesus Christ, history cannot unfold as more of the same. The new has come. Those who follow Christ are called to live in the newness of God's reign in the world, a world which has not yet recognized its rightful Lord.

It was precisely because Jesus lived utterly under the reign of God that he was crucified. The cross was the point of contact, the Ground Zero, of conflict between the present age and the age to come. Crucifixion was the inevitable result of living in light of the future in the present world. To live under the reign of God in the presence of those who exercise dominion over the powers and peoples of the world presents a threat that is not taken lightly. In the cross is seen the outcome of, not just the conviction that no one can serve two masters, but the determination to utterly submit to God as Master and Sovereign. To submit to God in such a way requires a willingness to live according to the standards of the world to come – to love defenselessly, serve indiscriminately, forgive persistently – without regard to the pride, preferences or interests of the powers of the present world. To live in this way leaves no room for the preservation of hostile divisions or the use of deadly force but demands a willingness to share in the sufferings of God in Christ.

The future age is not immediately apparent in the cross alone. It is only with the resurrection that it becomes clear. The resurrection is the vindication of the way of the cross, the way of self-sacrificing nonviolent love. It is the resurrection that most boldly and articulately declares that the cross is not the defeat of idealistic love and naïve good intentions but the unmasking of and triumph over the self-serving realms of this world and the power of sin and death. The resurrection explodes the confidence of those who embrace violence as they calculate consequences – "it is better that one man die than the whole nation perish" (John 11: 50). At the same time it confirms the incalculable capacity of God to use faithful obedience that is heedless of outcomes in order to attain divine ends. The resurrection demands confidence, not in human achievement but in the grace and power of God. The future is shown in the resurrection of Jesus Christ and this glorious event calls all who believe to live toward that future with faith – not in themselves but in the working of God.

As Campbell failed to be sufficiently cross-centered in his Christ-centeredness, so too did he insufficiently emphasize the resurrection in his eschatology. The assumption that the difference between defeat and triumph, failure and success can immediately be recognized is challenged by the eschatological act of God in the resurrection of Jesus Christ. From a purely human perspective, the cross was utter defeat, the tragic culmination of a nonviolent life in a violent world. The resurrection, however, is God's vindication of the way of the cross in the life of Christ. It is only because of the resurrection that it can be known that the nonviolent love demonstrated in the life of Jesus is more than a failed experiment in naïve goodwill. The resurrection proclaims that the truth of who God is for us and how God wants us to be toward each other is found in the faithfully defenseless life of Jesus. Hence, our willingness to use deadly force in order to achieve the victories we think necessary is put into question. Instead, we are to follow Christ – leaving the future in the hands of the God who brings life from the grave.

Nonviolence is to be practiced, not because we are convinced that it works to achieve good ends in any immediately observable and measurable way. Rather the conviction that God works, as demonstrated in the resurrection of

Jesus, undergirds Christian nonviolence. So long as we are convinced that the historical results we desire for our nation, our cause, or ourselves should arbitrate the decisions we make about violence, we will trust ourselves rather than trust the God who raised Jesus from the dead. The practice of nonviolence requires that we relinquish our imagined control over consequences and rely instead, upon the eschatological power of God. Violence can be seen as an option – even if it is limited to being a "necessary" last resort – only when we insist that we know what victory looks like and that we are responsible for insuring it is achieved. In contract, the resurrection is a sign of promise that points beyond human effectiveness or lack of effectiveness, success or defeat, to the death-defying power of God.

The resurrection does play a somewhat indirect role in Campbell's pacifist thought. For him the reign of Heaven, the resurrected Christ's reign over the church, shapes both motive and vision. It "draws heavenly feelings, desires and aims...and to heaven it leads."[33] Again, acceptance of Campbell's post-millennial eschatology is not necessary in order to affirm with him that the church is called to conform to the standards of heaven. The ethical significance of eschatology is not so much found in answering the question of *when* but *what*. In praying with Jesus, "Thy kingdom come, thy will be done on earth as it is in heaven," at issue is not the *when* of the millennium but the *what* – i.e., the will of God. As Jesus calls our attention to the kingdom of God, so, too, our attention must be directed to Jesus to learn what sort of life is fitting for the kingdom. In him we see the reality of the kingdom as he does God's will "on earth as it is in heaven." In Christ we are shown the kingdom in words of truth, acts of compassion and nonviolent love. By following him we live toward the kingdom that is coming and the church becomes a sign of the future.

The question for those who would be disciples of Jesus Christ is: "How can we participate in violence or war if we live lives suitable for and reflective of the kingdom of God?" If the kingdom of God is, indeed, a reign of harmony, peace and righteousness, what room can there be for killing and destruction in the life of the disciple? Must the pressures and conflicts of the present realm require Christians to compromise those behaviors appropriate for the reign of God in order to achieve desired ends in the world?

The issue here is not one of ushering God's kingdom into the world by means of social reform and ethical action. It is not by the good efforts of humans that God's kingdom comes but only by divine grace and power. Any realm dependent upon human achievement is bound to be something other than the kingdom of God. The rule of God brings about ethical behavior; ethical behavior does not produce the kingdom of God. The proleptic presence of the kingdom of God in the life and message of Jesus Christ gives rise to the anticipatory behavior in disciples as they live as church, which bears witness to the future kingdom of God.

The vision of the future offered in the resurrection and conveyed in scripture is not merely the expression of the dreams and aspirations of the human heart. Rather it is the result of the dependable promises of God. It is in these promises that Christians have confidence and are urged "to hold fast the confession of our hope without wavering, for he who promised is faithful" (Hebrews 10: 23). Life faithfully lived in hope is shaped by that hope, not just in inward attitude and deposition but in behavior. The actions of the hopeful life embodies what it envisions. This sort of life is lived, not strictly in response to the realities of the present, but in anticipation of and as witness to the promised future. Despite all evidence to the contrary, faithful hope assets that the future is in God's hands and behaves accordingly.

Whatever the shortcomings in Campbell's pacifism that may be legitimately criticized, still his views are worthy of careful attention, especially by those who align themselves with the American religious movement he helped shape. Certainly Campbell does not deserve to be revered without qualification and his views do not merit loyalty without critical scrutiny. But even more, there is no warrant for ignoring the thinking of the best mind among the earliest Disciples on the tremendously important matters of war and peace. As Campbell's thought challenged those of his time, his views should continue to challenge anyone who is concerned, as he was, for the faithfulness of the church in a fragmented world.

## Notes

1. H. Richard Niebuhr, *The Kingdom of God in America* (New York: Harper, 1937), 1.
2. *Millennial Harbinger*, 1830, 304, 309.
3. *The Evidences of Christianity: A Debate*, 409.
4. ibid., 410.
5. ibid., 403.
6. ibid., 409.
7. ibid., 411.
8. This has been ably and exhaustively demonstrated in relation to the writings of Paul by Michael J. Gorman, *Cruciformity: Paul's Narrative Spirituality of the Cross* (Grand Rapids: Eerdmans, 2001.)
9. ibid., 392.
10. Luke Timothy Johnson, *Living Jesus: Learning the Heart of the Gospel* (New York: Harper San Francisco, 1999), 200.
11. Campbell, *The Christian System*, 55.
12. ibid., 56.
13. *Millennial Harbinger*, 1848, 365.
14. ibid.
15. I've written about this more extensively in "Civil Religion and the Ecumenical Endeavor," *Word and World*, VIII / 3 (Summer, 1988), 252 - 264.
16. Stanley Hauerwas, *Peaceable Kingdom: A Primer in Christian Ethics* (Notre Dame, Indiana: University of Notre Dame Press, 1983), 102.
17. *Millennial Harbinger.*, 1862, 529.
18. *Christian System*, 269
19. ibid., Campbell makes a point of observing that the words "a holy and royal priesthood" are drawn from 1 Peter 2: 5, "and this is addressed to all the brethren dispensed in Pontus, Galatia, Cappadocia, Asia and Bithynia."
20. ibid.,273.
21. William T. Cavanaugh, *Theopolitical Imagination: Discovering the Liturgy as a Political Act in an Age of Global Consumerism* (London: T&T Clark, 2001), 50f.
22. Harold Lunger, 250.
23. *Millennial Harbinger*, 1848, 385.
24. ibid., 382.
25. Audrey R. Chapman, *Faith, Power, and Politics* (New York: The Pilgrim Press, 1991).
26. *Christianity Today*, 45/15 (3 Dec 2001), 17.
27. I addressed these matters in more detail in "Dealing Responsibly with Power: A Pacifist Perspective" *Cross Currents*, XXXVI/1 (Spring, 1986), 74 – 84.
28. *Millennial Harbinger*, 1853, 106.
29. *The Christian System*, 126.
30. ibid., 134.
31. *Millennial Harbinger*, 1841, 9.
32. ibid., 98.
33. *The Evidences of Christianity: A Debate*, 397.

# Appendix

# Alexander Campbell's Address on War

## Given at Wheeling, VA 1848 Published in the *Millennial Harbinger* July 1848, 361-386.

Ladies and gentlemen, has one Christian nation a right to wage war against another Christian nation?

On propounding to myself, and much more to you, my respected auditors, this momentous question so affecting the reputation and involving the destiny of our own country and that of the Christian world, I confess that I would rather shrink from its investigation than approach it with full confidence in my ability to examine it with that intelligence and composure so indispensable to a satisfactory decision. With your indulgence, however, I will attempt, if not to decide the question, at least to assist those who, like myself, have often and with intense interest reflected on the desolations and horrors of war, as indicated in the sacrifice of human life, the agonies of surviving relatives, the immense expenditures of a people's wealth and the inevitable deterioration of public morals invariably attendant on its existence and career. If with Dr. Dick, of Scotland, we should put down its slain victims to the minimum of 14,000,000,000; or with Burke, of Ireland, at the maximum of 35,000,000,000; or take the mean of 24,500,000,000, what imagination could picture all the miseries and agonies inflicted upon the slain and upon their surviving relatives and friends? And who could compute the wealth expended in the support of those immense armies whose butchered millions can never be exactly computed? If Great Britain alone, from the revolution in 1688 to the overthrow of Napoleon in 1815, during her 7 years' war, occupying 65 years of 127, expended the sum of 2,023,000,000 pounds (more than

$10,100,000,000) – a sum much more easily expressed than comprehended by even the most accomplished financier – how can we compute the aggregate expenditures of all the battles fought and wars carried on during a period of some 5,000 years? Yet these millions slain and these millions expended are the least items in its desolations to the mind of an enlightened Christian philanthropist. When we attempt to reflect upon one human being in the amplitude and magnitude of his whole destiny in a world that has no limit and also survey the capacities and susceptibilities of his nature according to the Christian revelation, how insignificant are the temporal and passing results of any course of action compared with those which know neither measure nor end. How important, then, it is that in investigating a subject whose bearings on society arithmetic cannot compute nor language express we approach it with a candid and unprejudiced temper and examine it with a profound and concentrated devotion of our minds to all that history records, philosophy teaches, and religion enjoins.

But, before entering upon the proper examination of this question, it may be of much importance to a satisfactory issue that we examine the terms in which it is expressed. More than half the discussions and controversies of every age are mere logomachies, verbose wranglings about the terminology of the respective combatants; and more than half the remainder might be compressed into a very diminutive size, if, in the beginning, the parties would agree on the real issue, on the proper terms to express and define them.

As public faith or commercial credit, founded upon an equivocal currency, on its exposure suddenly shrinks into ruinous dimensions, at once blighting the hopes and annihilating the fortune of many a bold adventurer, so many a false and dangerous position, couched in ambiguous terms, when pruned of its luxuriant verbiage, divested of its captivating but delusive elocution, and presented in an intelligible, definite, and familiar attitude, is at once reprobated as unworthy of our reception and regard.

On comparing the literature and science of the current age with those of former times, we readily discover how much we owe to a more rigid analysis and a more scrupulous adoption of the technical terms and phrases of the old schools, to which the whole world at one time looked up as the only fountains of wisdom and learning. When submitted to the test of a more enlightened criticism many of their most popular and somewhat cabalistic terms and phrases have been demonstrated to be words without just or appropriate ideas, and have been "nailed to the counter" as spurious coin; others, however, like pure metal in antique forms, have been sent to the mint, recast, and made to receive the impress of a more enlightened and accomplished age.

The rapid progress and advancement of modern science is, I presume, owing to a more rational and philosophical nomenclature and to the more general use of the inductive system of reasoning, rather than to any superior talent or more aspiring genius possessed either by our contemporaries or our immediate predecessors.
Politics, morals, and religion – the most deservedly engrossing themes of every age – are, in this respect, unfortunately, behind the other sciences and arts cultivated at the present day. We are, however, pleased to see a growing conviction of the necessity of a more apposite, perspicuous, and philosophical verbal apparatus in several departments of science, and especially to witness some recent efforts to introduce a more improved terminology in the sciences of government, morality, and religion.

To apply these preliminary remarks to the question of this evening, it is important to note with particular attention the popular terms in which we have expressed it, viz.:

"Has one Christian nation a right to wage war against another Christian nation?"

We have prefixed no epithet to war or to right, while we have to the word "nation." We have not defined the war as offensive or defensive. We have not defined the right as human or divine. But we have chosen, from the custom of the age, to prefix Christian to nation. The reasons for this selection and arrangement of terms shall appear as we proceed.

First, then, had we prefixed the word "offensive" to the word war, we would, on proving that a Christian nation had no right to wage an offensive war, be obliged to institute another question, and to ask, "Can a Christian nation wage a defensive war against another Christian nation?" thereby implying that one Christian nation might be the aggressor and another the aggrieved. But we cannot without great difficulty imagine such a thing as a Christian nation carrying on an aggressive war. We, therefore, simplify the discussion by placing in the proposition the naked term "war." Nor shall we spend our time in discussing the political right of one nation to wage war against another nation, and then ask whether they have a divine right. Indeed, the latter generally implies the former; for, if a nation has a divine right, it either has or may have a political or moral right to do so.

But we must inquire into the appropriateness of the term "Christian" prefixed to nation – for popular use has so arranged these terms – and the controversy, either expressly or impliedly, as nowadays occasionally conducted in this country, is, Has one Christian nation a right to wage war on another Christian nation? We have, indeed, had for many centuries past, many nations called Christian nations; but we must fearlessly ask, at what font were they baptized? Who were there godfathers? In what record are their sponsors registered? Aye, these, indeed, are preliminary questions that demand a grave and profound consideration. That there are many nations that have Christian communities in them is a proposition that we most cheerfully and thankfully admit. By a common figure of speech, we also give to that which contains anything the name of the thing contained in it. Thus, rhetorically, we call one edifice a college; another, a bank, a third, a church; not because the brick and mortar, the plank and nails, constitute a college, a bank, a church, but because these buildings contain these institutions. So we have – if anyone contend for the name – as many Christian nations as we have Christian communities in different nations, and as many Jewish nations as we have nations with Jewish synagogues in them, and as many Mohammedan nations as we have nations containing mosques in them. But, according to this rhetorical figure, we may have a Christian and a Mohammedan nation, in one and the same nation, as we sometimes find both a Jewish and a Christian synagogue in the same nation. But a rhetorical Christian nation and a proper and unfigurative Christian nation are very different entities. A proper literal Christian nation is not found in any country under the whole heavens. There is, indeed, one Christian nation, composed of all the Christian communities and individuals in the whole earth.

The Apostle Peter, in one letter addressed to all the Christians scattered throughout Pontus, Galatia, Cappadocia, Asia, and the Bithynia, though "strangers" or aliens in these respective nations, calls them collectively "a holy nation, a royal priesthood, a peculiar people." In strict logical and grammatical truth there is not, of all the nations of the earth, one properly called a Christian nation. Therefore, we have never had as yet one Christian nation waging war against another Christian nation. Before anyone, then, no matter what his learning or talents may be, can answer the great interrogatory now in discussion, he must form a clear and well defined conception of what constitutes a nation and what constitutes a Christian.

We have very high Roman authority for defining a nation, from nascor. Pardon me for quoting it: "*Genus hominum qui non aliunde venerunt, sed ibi nati sunt*"; which, in our vernacular, means a race or tribe of men who have not come abroad but live where they were born. Being a Roman word, derived from natural birth, a Roman author has the best right to define it. Now, a Christian is not one born where he lives; he is born from above, as all Christians of all parties admit. Therefore, no nation, as such, as respects either its natural birth or its constitution, can with any show of truth or reason be called a Christian nation. When anyone produces the annals of a nation whose constitution was given by Jesus Christ, and whose citizens are all born of God spiritually, as well as of man physically, I will at once call it, in good faith, without a figure, a true, proper, and literal Christian nation.

Now, although we have this advantage, which no one can take from us, and conceded, too, by all the literary and Christian authorities in Christendom, we will not build on it alone, nor at all. We will not have it said that we carry our definition by a grammatical or rhetorical decision of the great question. We appeal to all our public documents, without regard to party. We appeal to all our elementary and most profound writers on the subject of nationality. Nay, we appeal to the common views of this whole community. Have we not a church and a state in every State in the Union and in every European nation? Do not all belong to the state or nation, and a part only, and that often a small part, to the church? Is not the bond of political union blood, or naturalization? Is not the bond of union in the Christian kingdom faith, or the new birth? What nation is there whose citizens, or a majority of them, are Christians. Not one, even in profession.

But there is a reflex light of Christianity, a moralizing and a civilizing influence as well as a direct and soul-redeeming radiance, which imparts to those nations that have the oracles of God a higher standard of moral excellence, a more discriminating conscientiousness, and a more elevated national character which, in contrast with pagan nations, obtains for them the honorary distinction of Christian nation. Still, as nations, or states, the spirit and character of the nation are anti-Christian. A community of Jews in New York or New Orleans, even were they naturalized citizens of the United States, would not impart to those cities an American or Gentile spirit, nor would they impart to our Nation a Jewish spirit or character. They would still be Jews and we Americans.

The American Nation as a nation is no more in spirit Christian than were Greece and Rome when the apostle planted churches in Corinth, Athens, or in the metropolis of the empire, with Caesar's household in it. Roman policy, valor, bravery, gallantry, chivalry are of as much praise, admiration, and glory in Washington and London as they were in the very center of the pagan world in the days of Julius or Augustus Caesar. We worship our heroes because of their martial and Roman virtue. Virtue in the Roman language was only a name for bravery or courage. Such was its literal meaning. With a Roman it was queen of all the graces and of all moral excellencies. It raised from plebian to patrician rank and created military tribunes, decemvirs, triumvirs, dictators, consuls, kings, and emperors. With us it cannot make a king, but may, perhaps, a third time make for us a President. If, indeed, it does not yet make for us a king we shall blame the soil, not the culture. Kings cannot grow in America. But under our free and liberal institutions we can impart more than kingly power under a less offensive name.

But a Christian community is, by the highest authority, called a kingdom. He, however, who gave it this name, said to Caesar's representative, "My kingdom is not of this world. Had My kingdom been of this world, My servants would have fought, and I should not have been delivered to the Jews. But now is My kingdom not from hence." It is, then, decided, first, that we have no Christian nation or kingdom in the world, but that Christ has one grand kingdom composed of all the Christian communities in the world, of which He is Himself the proper sovereign, lawgiver, and king.

Having, then, no Christian nation to wage war against another Christian nation, the question is reduced to a more rational and simple form, and I trust it will be still more intelligible and acceptable in this form, viz.: Can Christ's kingdom or church in one nation wage war against His kingdom or church in another nation? With this simple view of the subject, where is the man so ignorant of the letter and spirit of Christianity as to answer this question in the affirmative? Is there a man of ordinary Bible education in this city or commonwealth who will affirm that Christ's church in England may of right wage war against Christ's church in America?

But I will be told that this form of the question does not meet the exact state of the case as now impinging the conscience of very man good men. While they will with an emphatic no negative the question as thus stated, they will in another form propound their peculiar difficulty:

"Suppose," say they, "England proclaims war against our Nation, or that our Nation proclaims war against England: Have we a right, as Christian men, to volunteer, or enlist, or, if drafted, to fight against England? Ought our motto to be, 'Our country, right or wrong'? Or has our Government a right to compel us to take up arms?"

This form of the question makes it important that we should have as clear and definite conceptions the word "right" as of any other word in the question before us. We must, then, have a little more definition. For the doctrine of right and wrong, so frequently spoken of by elementary political writers, I cannot say that I entertain a very high regard. Men without religious faith, being without an infallible guide, are peculiarly fond of abstractions. Led by imagination more than by reason, authority, or experience, they pride themselves in striking out for themselves and others a new path, rather than to walk in the old and long-frequented ways. They have a theory of man in society with political rights, and of man out of society with natural rights; but as they cannot agree as to the word "natural" prefixed to "right" – whether nature be a divinity or the cause of things – I will not now debate with them the question of natural rights, but will take the surer and well-established ground of a divine warrant, or a right founded on a divine annunciation.

Much, in all cases of any importance, depends on beginning right; and in a question upon right itself, everything depends upon that ultimate tribunal to which we make our appeal. In all questions involving the moral destinies of the world, we require more than hypothetical or abstract reasoning from principles merely assumed or conceded. We need demonstration, or what in this case of moral reasoning is the only substitute for it, oracular authority. All questions on morals and religion, all questions on the origin, relations, obligations, and destiny of man, can be satisfactorily decided only by an appeal to an infallible standard. I need not say that we all, I mean the civilized world, the great, the wise, the good of human kind, concede to the Bible this oracular authority; and, therefore, constitute it the ultimate reason and authority for each and every question of this sort. What, then, says the Bible on the subject of war? It certainly commended and authorized war among the Jews. God had given to man, ever since the flood, the right of taking away the life of man for one specified cause. Hence murderers, ever since the flood, were put to death by express divine authority. "He that sheds man's blood, by man shall his blood be shed." He gave authority only, however, to one family or nation, whose God and King he assumed to be. As soon as that family was developed into a nation, He placed it under His own special direction and authority. Its government has been properly called by Josephus, a distinguished Jew, a theocracy. It was not a republican, an aristocratical, or monarchical, but a theocratical government, and that, indeed, of the most absolute character, for certain high ends and purposes in the destinies of mankind – temporal, spiritual, and eternal. God was, therefore, in person the king, lawgiver, and judge of the Jewish nation.

It was not simply for desiring a king that God was at one time displeased with them. It was for asking a king like those of other nations, and thereby refusing God Himself and God alone as their king. Still, He never made their kings any more than viceroys. He, for many centuries, down to the end of the Old Testament history, held in His own hand the sovereignty of the nation. Hence the kings ruled for him, and the high priest, or some special prophet, was the Lord's mouth to them. Their kings were, therefore, unlike other kings. They truly, and only thy, of all the kings on earth, were "the Lord's anointed." The Jewish kingdom was emphatically a typical institution, prospective of a kingdom but not of this world, to be instituted in future times and to be placed under the special government of His only Son and Heir. Hence it came to pass that the enemies of Israel became typical of the enemies of Jesus Christ; and hence the temporal judgments inflicted on them were but shadows through which to set forth the spiritual and eternal judgments to be inflicted on the enemies of the Messiah's reign and kingdom. Whether, therefore, the enemies of the Jews fell in battle, or by any of the angels of death, it was God that slew them. Hence their kings and God's angels were but mere sheriffs, executing, as it were, the mandates of high heaven.

It is, however, important to reiterate that God gave to Noah, and through him to all his sons and successors in government, a right to take away, in civil justice, the life of a murderer. As the world of the ungodly, antecedent to the Deluge, during the first 500 years of Noah's life, was given to violence and outrage against each other, it became expedient to prevent the same violence and bloodshed after the flood; and for this purpose God gave to man, or the human race in Noah's family, the right to exact blood for blood from him who had deliberately and maliciously taken away the life of his fellow. Had not this been first ordained, no war, without a special divine commission, could have been sanctioned as lawful and right even under the Old Testament institution. Hence we may say that wars were first allowed by God against those who had first waged war against their fellows, and consequently, as viewed by God himself, they were murderers. The first and second wars was reported in the annals of the world were begun by the enemies of God and His people, and hence the reprisals made by Abraham and Moses are distinctly stated to have been occasioned by the enemies of God and His people.

But what is most important here and apposite to the occasion is that these wars waged by God's people in their typical character were waged under and in pursuance of a special divine commission. They were, therefore, right. For a divine precept authorizing anything to be done makes it right absolutely and forever. The Judge of all the earth can do only that, or command that to be done, which is right.

Let those, then, who now plead a *jus divinum*, a special divine warrant or right for carrying on war by the authority of the Lord Jesus Christ, produce a warrant from the present Monarch of the universe. What the God of Abraham did by Abraham, by Jacob, or by any of his sons, as the moral Governor of the world, before He gave up the scepter and the crown to His Son, Jesus Christ, is of no binding authority now. This is a point of much more importance than we can at present develop, and one which has been, so far as known to me, wholly slurred over in this great investigation. The very basis of the Christian religion is that Jesus Christ is now the Lord and King of both earth and heaven, and that His Father and our God no longer assumes to be either the lawgiver, judge, or king of the world. It is positively declared by Him that all legislative, judiciary, and executive power is now committed into the hands of One who is both our kinsman and God's only begotten Son. Two grand declarations that ought to revolutionize our whole views of civil government as respects its ultimate authority, and change some of our forms of legal justice, are wholly overlooked so far as they are of any practical value and importance. The first was announced by the Messiah immediately before His ascension into heaven; the other was publicly pronounced by an embassy from heaven immediately after His ascension. The former declares that "all authority" (exousia), all legislative, judiciary, and regal authority in heaven and earth is given to Jesus Christ; the other affirms that God has made Jesus, Lord and Christ, or anointed Him sovereign of the universe. Kings of the earth and courts of high judicature are all under Him, but they do not really acknowledge it; few of them, perhaps, know or believe the fact that Jesus Christ has been on the throne of the universe for more than 1,800 years. Hence, the courts of England and America, the two most enlightened nations in the world, are yet deistical in form, rather than Christian. In every place where they have the phrase, "In the name of God," they ought to have, "In the name of the Lord." This is the gist of the whole controversy between the friends and the enemies of war, on the part of the subjects of Christ's kingdom. The coronation of Jesus Christ in heaven as Lord of all, His investiture with all authority in heaven and earth, legislative, judiciary, and executive, is the annunciation, on the belief and public acknowledgment of which the first Christian church was founded in Jerusalem, where the throne of David was, in the month of June, 1,814 years ago, A.D. 34. God the Father, in propria persona, now neither judges nor punishes any person or nation, but has committed all judgment to His Son, now constituted head of the universe and judge of the living and the dead. This simplifies the question and leaves it to the judgment of all. It is this: Has the author and founder of the Christian religion enacted war or has He made it lawful and right for the subjects of His government to go to war against one another? Or, has He made it right for them to go to war against any nation, or for any national object, at the bidding of the present existent political authorities of any nation in Christendom?

The question is not whether, under the new administration of the universe, Christian communities have a right to wage war, in its common technical sense, against other communities – as the house of Judah against the house of Israel, both of the same religion, language, and blood. This is already, by almost universal consent, decided in the negative, probably only one society of professed Christians excepted. But the question is, May a Christian community, or the members of it, in their individual capacities, take up arms at all, whether aggressively or defensively, in any national conflict? We might, as before alleged, dispense with the words "aggressive" and "defensive";

for a mere grammatical, logical, or legal quibble will make any war either aggressive or defensive, just as the whim, caprice, or interest of an individual pleases. Napoleon, on his deathbed, declared that he had never engaged, during his whole career, in an aggressive war – that all his wars were very defensive. Yet all Europe regarded him as the most aggressive warrior of any age.

But the great question is: Can an individual, not a public functionary, morally do that in obedience to his government that he cannot do in his own case? Suppose the master of an apprenticed youth, or the master of a number of hired or even bond servants, should fall out with one of his neighbors about one of the lines of his plantation, because, as he imagined, his neighbor had trespassed upon his freehold in clearing or cultivating his lands. His neighbor refuses to retire within the precincts insisted on by the complainant; in consequence of which the master calls together his servants and proceeds to avenge himself or, as he alleges, to defend his property. As the controversy waxes hot, he commands his servants not only to burn and destroy the improvements made on the disputed territory but to fire upon his neighbor, his sons, and servants. They obey orders, and kill several of them. They are, however, finally taken into custody and brought to trial. An attorney for the servants pleads that those servants were bound to obey their master, and quotes these words from the Good Book: "Servants, obey in all things your masters according to the flesh." But, on the other side, it is shown that the "all things" enjoined are only "all things lawful." For this obedience is to be rendered "as to Christ"; and, again, "as the servants of Christ, doing the will of God from the heart." No judge or jury could do otherwise than condemn as guilty of murder servants thus acting. Now, as we all, in our political relations to the Government of our country, occupy positions at least inferior to that which a bond servant holds toward his master, we cannot of right as Christian men obey the powers that be in anything not in itself justifiable by the written law of the great King – our liege Lord and Master, Jesus Christ. Indeed, we may advance in all safety one step further, if it were necessary, and affirm that a Christian man can never of right be compelled to do that for the state, in defense of state rights, which he cannot of right do for himself in defense of his personal rights. No Christian man is commanded to love or serve his neighbor, his king, or sovereign more than he loves or serves himself. If this is conceded, unless a Christian man can go to war for himself, he cannot for the state.

We have already observed that the Jews were placed under a theocracy, that their kings were only vice-regents, and that they were a symbolic or typical nation adumbrative of a new relation and institution to be set up in "the fullness of time" under an administration of grace. In consequence of this arrangement, God was first revealed as the God of Abraham; and afterward, when He was about to make Himself known in all the earth, in contrast with the idols of the nations, He chose by Moses to call Himself the God of the Hebrews. As the custom then was, all nations had their gods, and by their wars judged and decided the claims and pretensions of their respective divinities. Esteeming the reputation and pretensions of their gods according to their success in war, that nation's god was the greatest and most to be venerated whose people were most successful and triumphant in battle. God, therefore, chose this method to reveal Himself as the God of the Hebrews. Hence He first poured out 10 plagues upon the gods of Egypt. The Egyptians worshipped everything from the Nile and its tenantry to the meanest insect in the land. He first, then, plagued their gods. Afterward, by causing the Jews to fight and destroy many nations in a miraculous manner, from the victory over Amalek to the fall of the cities and kings of ancient Palestine, He established His claims as supreme over all. Proceeding in this way, He fully manifested the folly of their idolatries and the omnipotence, greatness, and majesty of the God of the Jews.

The wars of pagan nations were, indeed, much more rational than those of our miscalled Christian nations. No two of these nations acknowledged the same dynasties of gods; and, therefore, having different gods, they could with much propriety test their claims by invoking them in battle. But two Christian nations both pray to one and the same God to decide their respective quarrels and yet will not abide by the decision; for success in war is not by any of them regarded as an end of all strife as to the right or justice of the demands of the victorious party. Did our present belligerent nations regard victory and triumph as a proof of the justice of their respective claims, they would in the manner of carrying on their wars prove themselves to be very great simpletons indeed; for why sacrifice their hundred millions of dollars and their fifty thousand lives in one or two years, when they could save these millions of men and money by selecting each one of their genuine simon-pure patriots and heroes and having them voluntarily to meet in single combat before a competent number of witnesses and encounter each other till one of them triumphed – and thus award, from heaven's own court of infallible rectitude, to the nation of the survivor the glory of a great national triumph both in heroism and justice? But this they dare not do, for these Christian nations are quite skeptical so far as faith in the justice of their own cause or in the right decision of their claims in the providence and moral government of God is concerned. To what purpose, we therefore ask, do they both appeal to the same God, when neither of them feels any obligation to abide His decision?

But as we are neither under a Jewish nor a Pagan government, but professedly, at least, under a Christian dispensation, we ought to hear what the present King of the Universe has enacted on this subject. The maxims of the Great Teacher and Supreme Philanthropist are, one would think, to be final and decisive on this great question. The Great Lawgiver addresses His followers in two very distinct respects: First, in reference to their duties to Him and their own profession, and then in reference to their civil rights, duties, and obligations.

So far as any indignity was offered to them or any punishment inflicted upon them as His followers, or for His name's sake, they were in no way to resent it. But in their civil rights He allows them the advantages of the protection of civil law, and for this cause enjoins upon them the payment of all their political dues, and to be subject to every ordinance of man of a purely civil nature, not interfering with their obligations to Him.

"If a heathen man, or persecutor, smite you on one cheek, turn to him the other also. If he compels you to go with him one mile, go two. If he sue thee at law, and take away thy coat, let him have thy mantle also," etc. These and whatever else of civil treatment they might receive, as Disciples of Christ, they must, for His sake, endure without resistance or resentment. But if in their citizen character or civil relations they are defrauded, maligned, or prosecuted, they might, and they did, appeal to Caesar. They paid tribute to civil magistrates that they might protect them; and therefore they might rightfully claim their protection. In this view of the matter, civil magistrates were God's ministers to the Christian "for good." And also, as God's ministers, they were revengers to execute wrath on those who did evil. Therefore, Christians are in duty bound to render to Caesar what is Caesar's, and to God what is God's – to reverence, honor, and support the civil magistrate, and, when necessary, to claim his protection. But as respects the life peculiar to a soldier, or the prosecution of a political war, they had no commandment. On the contrary, they were to live peaceably with all men to the full extent of their power. Their sovereign Lord, the King of Nations, is called "The Prince of Peace." How, then, could a Christian soldier, whose "shield" was faith, whose "helmet" was the hope of salvation, whose "breastplate" was righteousness, whose "girdle" was truth, whose "feet were shod with the preparation of the gospel of peace," and whose "sword" was that fabricated by the Holy Spirit, even "the word," a Hannibal, a Tamerlane, a Napoleon, or even a Victoria?

Jesus said, "All that take the sword shall perish by the sword." An awful warning! All that take it to support religion, it is confessed, have fallen by it; but it may be feared that it is not simply confined to that; for may I not ask the pages of universal history, have not all the nations created by the sword finally fallen by it? Should anyone say, "Some few of them yet stand," we respond, "All that have fallen also stood for a time; and are not those that now stand tottering just at this moment to their overthrow?" We have no doubt; it will prove in the end that nations and states founded by the sword shall fall by the sword.

When the Saviour, in His sententious and figurative style, indicating the trials just coming upon His friends, said, "You had better sell your outside garments and buy a sword," one present, understanding him literally, as some of the friends of war still do, immediately responded, "Lord, here are two swords." What did he say? "It is enough." Two swords for twelve apostles! Truly, they are dull scholars who thence infer that He meant they should literally use two swords to fight with! When asked by Pilate whether He was a king, He responded that He was born to be a king, but not a king of worldly type or character. Had He been such a king, his servants would, indeed, have used the sword. But His kingdom neither came nor stands by the sword. When first announced as a king by the Jewish prophets, more than seven centuries before He was born, the Spirit said of His reign, "He shall judge among the nations, and decide among many people. And they shall beat their swords into ploughshares, and their spears into pruning hooks; nation shall not lift up sword against nation, neither shall they learn war any more." (Isaiah 2:2-4.) Two prophets describe it in almost the same words. Micah, as well as Isaiah, says:

"Out of Zion shall go forth the law,
And the word of Jehovah from Jerusalem;
And He shall judge among many people.
And decide among strong nations afar off;
And they shall beat their swords into ploughshares,
And their spears into pruning-hooks;
Neither shall they any longer learn war;
But they shall sit every man under his vine,
And under his fig-tree, and none shall make him afraid;
For the mouth of Jehovah of hosts hath spoken it."

Such was, according to prophecy, such is, according to fact, the native influence and tendency of the Christian institution. The spirit of Christianity, then, is essentially pacific.

There is often a multiplication of testimony for display rather than for effect. And, indeed, the accumulation of evidence does not always increase its moral momentum. Nor is it very expedient on other considerations to labor a point that is generally, if not universally, admitted. That the genius and spirit of Christianity, as well as the letter of it, are admitted, on all hands, to be decidedly "peace on earth, and good will among men," needs no proof to anyone that has ever read the volume that contains it. But if anyone desires to place in contrast the gospel of Christ and the genius of war, let him suppose the chaplain of an army addressing the soldiers on the eve of a great battle, on performing faithfully their duty, from such passages as the following: "Love your enemies; bless them that curse you; do good to them that hate you, and pray for them that despitefully use you and persecute you, that you may be the children of your Father in Heaven, who makes his sun to rise upon the evil and the good, and sends his rain upon the just and the unjust."

Again, in our civil relations: "Recompense to no man evil for evil." "As much as lieth in you, live peaceably with all men." "Dearly beloved, avenge not yourselves; but rather give place to wrath." "If thine enemy hunger, feed him; if he thirst, give him drink." "Be not overcome of evil; but overcome evil with good." Would anyone suppose that he had selected a text suitable to the occasion? How would the commander in chief have listened to him? With what spirit would his audience have immediately entered upon an engagement? These are questions which every man must answer for himself, and which everyone can feel much better than express.

But a Christian man cannot conscientiously enter upon any business, nor lend his energies to any cause, which he does not approve; and in order to approve he must understand the nature and object of the undertaking. Now, how does this dictate of discretion, religion, and morality bear upon the case before us?

Nothing, it is alleged, more tends to weaken the courage of a conscientious soldier than to reflect upon the originating causes of wars and the objects for which they are prosecuted. These, indeed, are not always easily comprehended. Many wars have been prosecuted, and some have been terminated after long and protracted efforts, before the great majority of the soldiers themselves, on either side, distinctly understood what they were fighting for. Even in our country, a case of this sort has, it is alleged, very recently occurred. If, it is presumed, the true and proper causes of most wars were clearly understood and the real design for which they are prosecuted could be clearly and distinctly apprehended, they would, in most instances, miscarry for the want of efficient means of a successful prosecution.

A conviction of this sort, some years ago, occasioned an elaborate investigation of the real causes for which the wars of Christendom had been undertaken from the time of Constantine the Great down to the present century. From the results furnished the Peace Society of Massachusetts it appeared that, after subtracting a number of petty wars long since carried on and those waged by Christian nations with tribes of savages, the wars of real magnitude amounted in all to 286.

The origin of these wars, on a severe analysis, appeared to have been as follows: 22 for plunder and tribute; 44 for the extension of territory; 24 for revenge or retaliation; 6 for disputed boundaries; 8 respecting points of honor or prerogative; 6 for the protection or extension of commerce; 55 civil wars; 41 about contested titles to crowns; 30 under pretense of assisting allies; 23 for mere jealousy of rival greatness; 28 religious wars, including the Crusades. Not one for defense alone, and certainly not one that an enlightened Christian man could have given one cent for, in a voluntary way, much less have volunteered his services or enlisted into its ranks.

If the end alone justifies the means, what shall we think of the wisdom or the justice of war, or of the authors and prominent actors of these scenes? A conscientious mind will ask: did these 286 wars redress the wrongs, real of feigned, complained of? Did they in all cases, in a majority of the cases, or in a single case, necessarily determine the right side of the controversy? Did they punish the guilty, or the more guilty, in the ratio of their respective demerits? No one can, indeed, no one will, contend that the decision or termination of these wars naturally, necessarily, or even probably, decided the controversy so justly, so rationally, so satisfactorily as it could have been settled in any one case of the 286 by a third or neutral party.

War is not now, nor was it ever, a process of justice. It never was a test of truth – a criterion of right. It is either a mere game of chance or a violent outrage of the strong upon the weak. Need we any other proof that a Christian people can in no way whatever countenance a war as a proper means of redressing wrongs, of deciding justice, or of settling controversies among nations? On the common conception of the most superficial thinkers on this subject, not one of the 286 wars which have been carried on among the "Christian nation's" during 1,500 years was such as that an enlightened Christian man could have taken any part in it, because, as admitted, not one of them was for defense alone; in other words, they were all aggressive wars.

But to the common mind, as it seems to me, the most convincing argument against a Christian becoming a soldier may be drawn from the fact that he fights against an innocent person – I say an innocent person, so far as the cause of the war is contemplated. The men that fight are not the men that make the war. Politicians, merchants, knaves, and princes cause or make the war, declare the war, and hire men to kill for them those that may be hired on the other side to thwart their schemes of personal and family aggrandizement.

The soldiers on either side have no enmity against the soldiers on the other side, because with them they have no quarrel. Had they met in any other field, in their citizen dress, other than in battle array, they would, most probably have not only inquired after the welfare of each other, but would have tendered to each other their assistance if called for. But a red coat or a blue coat, a tri-colored or a two-colored cockade, is their only introduction to each other, and the signal that they must kill or be killed! If they think at all, they must feel that there is no personal alienation, or wrong, or variance between them. But they are paid so much for the job; and they go to work, as the day laborer to earn his shilling. Need I ask, how could a Christian man thus volunteer his services, or hire himself out for so paltry a sum, or for any sum, to kill to order his brother man who never offended him in word or deed? What infatuation! What consummate folly and wickedness! Well did Napoleon say, "War is the trade of barbarians"; and his conqueror, Wellington, "Men of nice scruples about religion have no business in the army or navy." The horrors of war only enhance the guilt of it; and these, alas, no one can depict in all their hideous forms.

By the "horrors of war" I do not mean the lightning and the thunder of the battlefield, the blackness and darkness of those dismal clouds of smoke, which like death's own pall, shroud the encounter; it is not the continual roar of its cannon, nor the agonizing shrieks and groans of fallen battalions, of wounded and dying legions; nor is it, at the close of the day, the battlefield itself, covered with the gore and scattered limbs of butchered myriads, with here and there a pile, a mountain heap of slain heroes in the fatal pass, mingled with the wreck of broken arms, lances, helmets, swords, and shattered firearms, amidst the pavement of fallen balls that have completed the work of destruction, numerous as hailstones after the fury of the storm; nor, amidst these, the sight of the wounded lying upon one another, weltering in their blood, imploring assistance, importuning an end of their woes by the hand of a surviving soldier, invoking death as the only respite from excruciating torments. But this is not all; for the tidings are at length carried to their respective homes. Then come the bitter wail of widows and orphans, the screams and the anguish of mothers and sisters deprived forever of the consolations and hopes that clustered round the anticipated return of those so dear to them, that have perished in the conflict.

But even these are not the most fearful desolations of war. Where now are the 200,000 lost by England in our Revolutionary War; the 70,000 who fell at Waterloo and Quatre-Bros; the 80,000 at Borodino; the 300,000 at Arbela; or where the 15,000,000 Goths destroyed by Justinian in 20 years; the 32,000,000 by Genghis

Khan in 41 years; the 60,000,000 slain by the Turks; the 80,000,000 by the Tartars, hurried away to judgment in a paroxysm of wrath, amid the fury of the passions? What can we think of their eternal destiny?[1] Besides all these, how many have died in captivity? How many an unfortunate exile or captive might, with a French prisoner, sing of woes like these, or even greater? :

I dwelt upon the willowy banks of Loire;
I married one who from my boyish days
Had been my playmate. One morn – I'll ne'er forget –
While choosing out the fairest twigs
To warp a cradle for our child unborn,
We heard the tidings that the conscript lot
Had fallen on me. It came like a death knell!
The mother perish'd; but the babe survived;
And, ere my parting day, his rocking couch
I made complete, and saw him sleeping, smile –
The smile that play'd erst on the cheek or her
Who lay clay cold. Alas! the hour soon came
That forced my fetter'd arms to quit my child!
And whether now he lives to deck with flowers
The sod upon his mother's grave, or lies
Beneath it by her side, I ne'er could learn.
I think he's gone; and now I only wish
For liberty and home, that I may see,
And stretch myself and die upon their grave!

But these, multiplied by myriads, are but specimens of the countless millions slain, the solitary exiles, the lonely captives. They tell the least portion of the miseries of war. Yet even these say to the Christian, "How can you become a soldier? How countenance and aid this horrible work of death?"

For my own part, and I am not alone in this opinion, I think that the moral desolations of war surpass even its horrors. And amongst these I do not assign the highest place to the vulgar profanity, brutality, and debauchery of the mere soldier, the professional and licensed butcher of mankind, who, for his $8 a month or his 10 sous per day, hires himself to lay waste a country, to pillage, burn, and destroy the peaceful hamlet, the cheerful village, or the magnificent city, and to harass, wound, and destroy his fellow man, for no other consideration than his paltry wages, his daily rations, and the infernal pleasure of doing it, anticipating hereafter "the stupid stares and loud huzzas" of monsters as inhuman and heartless as himself. And were it not for the infatuation of public opinion and popular applause, I would place him, as no less to be condemned, beside the vain and pompous volunteer, who for his country, "right or wrong," hastens to the theater of war for the mere plaudits of admiring multitudes, ready to cover himself with glory, because he has aided an aspirant to a throne or paved the way to his own election to reign over a humbled and degraded people.

I make great allowance for false education, for bad taste, for the contagion of vicious example; still, I cannot view those deluded by such sophistry, however good their motives, as deserving anything from contemporaries or posterity except compassion and forgiveness. Yet, behold its influence on mothers, sisters, and relatives; note its contagion, its corruption of public taste. See the softer sex allured, fascinated by the halo of false glory thrown around these worshipped heroes! See them gazing with admiration on the "tinselled trapping," the "embroidered ensigns," of him whose profession it is to make widows and orphans by wholesale! Sometimes their hands are withdrawn from works of charity to decorate the warriors' banners and to cater to these false notions of human glory! Behold, too, the young mother arraying her proud boy "with cap and feather, toyed with a drum and sword, training him for the admired profession of a man killer."

This is not all. It is not only at home, in the nursery, and infant school that this false spirit is inspired. Our schools, our academies, our colleges echo and reecho with the fame of an Alexander, a Caesar, a Napoleon, a Wellington. Forensic eloquence is full of the fame of great heroes, of military chieftains, of patriotic deliverers whose memory must be kept forever verdant in the affections of a grateful posterity, redeemed by their patriotism or rescued from oppression by their valor.

The pulpit, too, must lend its aid in cherishing the delusion. There is not infrequently heard a eulogium on some fallen hero, some church service for the mighty dead, thus desecrating the religion of the Prince of Peace by causing it to minister as the handmaid of war. Not only are prayers offered up by pensioned chaplains on both sides of the field even amid the din of arms, but Sabbath after Sabbath, for years and years, have the pulpits on one side of a sea or river and those on the other side resounded with prayers for the success of rival armies, as if God could hear them both and make each triumphant over the other, guiding and commissioning swords and bullets to the heads and hearts of their respective enemies.

And not only this; but even the churches in the Old World, and sometimes in the new, are ornamented with the sculptured representations of more military heroes than of saints – generals, admirals, and captains who "gallantly fought" and "gloriously fell" in the service of their country. It is not only in Westminster Abbey or in St. Paul's that we read their eulogiums and see their statues, but even in some of our own cities we find St. Paul driven out of the church to make room for generals and commodores renowned in fight. And, last of all, in consummation of the moral desolation of war we sometimes have an illumination – even a thanksgiving – rejoicing that God has caused ten or twenty thousand of our enemies to be sent down to Tartarus and has permitted myriads of widows and orphans to be made at the bidding of some chieftain or of some aspirant to a throne.

But it would exhaust too much time to speak of the inconsistencies of the Christian world on this single subject of war, or to trace to their proper fountains the general misconceptions of the people on their political duties and that of their governments. This would be the work of volumes – not of a single address. The most enlightened of our ecclesiastic leaders seem to think that Jesus Christ governs the nations as God governed the Jews. They cannot separate, even in this land, the church and state. They still ask for a Christian national code.

If the world were under a politico-ecclesiastic king or president, it would, indeed, be hard to find a model for him in the New Testament. Suffice it to say that the church, and the church only, is under the special government and guardianship of our Christian King. The nations, not owning Jesus Christ, are disowned by him; He leaves them to themselves, to make their own institutions, as God anciently did all nations but the Jews. He holds them in abeyance, and as in providence, so in government, He makes all things work together for the good of His people, restrains the wrath of their enemies, turns the counsels and wishes of kings as He turns the rivers, but never condescends to legislate for the bodies of men, or their goods or chattels, who withhold from Him their consciences and their hearts. He announces the fact that it is by His permission, not always with His approbation, that kings reign and that princes decree justice, and commands his people politically to obey their rulers and to respect the ordinances of kings, that "they may lead quiet and peaceable lives in all godliness and honesty." And where the Gospel of Christ comes to kings and rulers, it addresses them as men in common with other men, commanding them to repent of their sins, to submit to His government and to discharge their relative duties according to the morality and piety inculcated in His code. If they do this, they are a blessing to His people as well as an honor to themselves. If they do not, He will hold them to a reckoning, as other men, from which there is neither escape nor appeal. What Shakespeare says is as true of kings as of their subjects:

> War is a game that, were their subjects wise,
> Kings would not play at.

For, were both kings and people wise, wars would cease, and nations would learn war no more.

But how are all national disputes to be settled? Philosophy, history, the Bible, teach that all disputes, misunderstandings, alienations are to be settled, heard, tried, adjudicated by impartial, that is, by disinterested, umpires. No man is admitted to be a proper judge in his own case. Wars never make amicable settlements, and seldom, if ever, just decisions of points at issue. We are obliged to offer preliminaries of peace at last. Nations must meet by their representatives, stipulate and re-stipulate, hear and answer, compare and decide.

In modern times we terminate hostilities by a treaty of peace. We do not make peace with power and lead. It is done by reason, reflection, and negotiation. Why not employ these at first? But it is alleged that war has long been, and must always be, the ultima ratio regum – the last argument of those in power. For ages a father inquisitor was the strong argument for orthodoxy; but light has gone abroad and he has lost his power. Illuminate the human mind on this subject also, create a more rational and humane public opinion, and wars will cease.

But, it is alleged, all will not yield to reason or justice. There must be compulsion. Is war then the only compulsory measure? Is there no legal compulsion? Must all personal misunderstandings be settled by the sword?

Why not have a by-law-established umpire? Could not a united national court be made as feasible and as practicable as a United States court? Why not, as often proposed, and as eloquently, ably, and humanely argued, by the advocates of peace, have a congress of nations and a high court of nations for adjudicating and terminating all international misunderstandings and complaints, redressing and remedying all wrongs and grievances?

There is not, it appears to me, a physical or a rational difficulty in the way. But I do not now argue the case. I merely suggest this expedient, and will always vote correspondingly, for reasons as good and as relevant as I conceive them to be humane and beneficial.

To sum up the whole we argue:

(1) The right to take away the life of the murderer does not of itself warrant war, inasmuch as in that case none but the guilty suffer, whereas in war the innocent suffer not only with, but often without, the guilty. The guilty generally make war and the innocent suffer from its consequences.

(2) The right given to the Jews to wage war is not vouchsafed to any other nation, for they were under a theocracy, and were God's sheriff to punish nations; consequently no Christian can argue from the wars of the Jews in justification or in extenuation of

the wars of Christendom. The Jews had a Divine precept and authority; no existing nation can produce such a warrant.

(3) The prophecies clearly indicate that the Messiah himself would be "the Prince of Peace," and that under his reign "wars should cease" and "nations study it no more."

(4) The gospel, as first announced by the angels, is a message that results in producing "peace on earth and good will among men."

(5) The precepts of Christianity positively inhibit war – by showing that "wars and fightings come from men's lusts" and evil passions, and by commanding Christians to "follow peace with all men.

(6) The beatitudes of Christ are not pronounced on patriots, heroes, and conquerors but on peacemakers, on whom is conferred the highest rank and title in the universe: "Blessed are the peacemakers, for they shall be called the sons of God.

(7) The folly of war is manifest in the following particulars: First. It can never be the criterion of justice of a proof of right. Second. It can never be a satisfactory end of the controversy. Third. Peace is always the result of negotiation, and treaties are its guaranty and pledge.

(8) The wickedness of war is demonstrated in the following particulars:
First. Those who are engaged in killing their brethren, for the most part, have no personal cause of provocation whatever.
Second. They seldom, or never, comprehend the right or the wrong of the war. They, therefore, act without the approbation of conscience.
Third. In all wars the innocent are punished with the guilty.
Fourth. They constrain the soldier to do for the state that which, were he to do it for himself, would, by the law of the state, involve forfeiture of his life.
Fifth. They are the pioneers of all other evils to society, both moral and physical. In the language of Lord Brougham, "Peace, peace, peace! I abominate war as un-Christian. I hold it the greatest of human curses. I deem it to include all others – violence, blood, rapine, fraud, everything that can deform the character, alter the nature, and debase the name of man." Or with Joseph Bonaparte, "War is but organized barbarism – an inher-

itance of the savage state," With Franklin I, therefore, conclude, "There never was a good war, or a bad peace."

No wonder, then, that for two or three centuries after Christ all Christians refused to bear arms. So depose Justin Martyr, Tatian, Clement of Alexandria, Tertullian, Origen, and so forth.

In addition to all these considerations, I further say, were I not a Christian, as a political economist even, I would plead this cause. Apart from the mere claims of humanity, I would urge it on the ground of sound national policy.

Give me the money that's been spent in wars and I will clear up every acre of land in the world that ought to be cleared, drain every marsh, subdue every desert, fertilize every mountain and hill, and convert the whole earth into a continuous series of fruitful fields, verdant meadows, beautiful villas, hamlets, towns, cities, standing along smooth and comfortable highways and canals, or in the midst of luxuriant and fruitful orchards, vineyards, and gardens, full of fruits and flowers, redolent with all that pleases the eye and regales the senses of man. I would found, furnish, and endow as many schools, academies, and colleges as would educate the whole human race, would build meeting houses, public halls, lyceums, and furnish them with libraries adequate to the wants of a thousand millions of human beings.

Beat your swords into plowshares, your spears into pruning hooks, convert your warships into missionary packets, your arsenals and munitions of war into Bibles, school books, and all the appliances of literature, science, and art, and then ask, "What would be wanting on the part of man to 'make the wilderness and solitary peace glad,' to cause 'the desert to rejoice and blossom as the rose,' to make our hills 'like Carmel and Sharon,' and our valleys as 'the garden of God'?" All this being done, I would doubtless have a surplus for some new enterprise.

On reviewing the subject in the few points only that I have made and with the comparatively few facts I have collected, I must confess that I both wonder at myself and am ashamed to think that I have never before spoken out my views, nor even written an essay on this subject. True, I had, indeed, no apprehension of ever again seeing or even hearing of a war in the United States. It came upon me so suddenly, and it so soon became a party question, that, preserving, as I do, a strict neutrality between party politics, both in my oral and written addresses on all subjects, I could not for a time decide whether to speak out or be silent. I finally determined not to touch the subject till the war was over. Presuming that time to have arrived, and having resolved that my first essay from my regular course, at any foreign point should be on this subject, I feel that I need offer no excuse, ladies and gentlemen, for having called your attention to the matter in hand. I am sorry to think – very sorry indeed to be only of the opinion – that probably even this much published by me some three years or even two years ago, might have saved some lives that since have been thrown away in the desert – some hot-brained youths :

Whose limbs, unburied on the shore,
Devouring dogs or hungry vultures tore.

We have all a deep interest in the question; we can all do something to solve it; and it is everyone's duty to do all the good he can. We must create a public opinion on this subject. We should inspire a pacific spirit and urge on all proper occasions the chief objections to war. In the language of the eloquent Grimké, we must show that "the great objection to war is not so much the number of lives and the amount of property it destroys, as its moral influence on nations and individuals. It creates and perpetuates national jealousy, fear, hatred, and envy. It arrogates to itself the prerogative of the Creator alone – to involve the innocent multitude in the punishment of the guilty few. It corrupts the moral taste and hardens the heart; cherishes and strengthens the base and violent passions; destroys the distinguishing features of Christian charity – its universality and its love of enemies; turns into mockery and contempt the best virtue of Christians – humility; weakens the sense of moral obligation; banishes the spirit of improvement, usefulness, and benevolence; and inculcates the horrible maxim that murder and robbery are matters of state expediency."

Let everyone, then, who fears God and loves man put his hand to the work; and the time will not be far distant when:

No longer hosts encountering hosts
Shall crowds of slain deplore:
They'll hang the trumpet in the hall,
And study war no more.

# Notes

[1] "War a Destroyer of Souls," (a tract of the Peace Society.)

## NOTES

# Index


## A

Address on War
5 23, 33, 39, 56, 98, 108, 112, 139
Allen, William 69, 104
American Peace Society
22, 45, 46, 60, 62, 70-71,
84, 85, 88-89, 103-105, 130
Anabaptists 11, 18, 69
Armstrong, William 75
Augsburg Confession 10

## B

Bacon, Francis 41
Ballou, Adin 105
Baptists 10, 11
Beckwith, George 105
Blanshard, Joshua P. 70
Book of Discipline 19
Burritt, Elihur 61

## C

Calvin, John 41, 111, 115
Campbell, Thomas 10, 18, 88
capital punishment
39, 73, 102-113, 115, 121
Channing, William Ellery 70
*Christian Baptist, The*
17, 27, 28, 42, 57, 58, 85,
86, 91, 100, 113
Christian community 37, 146, 148
Church of England 10
Civil War
11, 17, 35, 64-66, 68, 82, 91
Constantine 36, 152
Creath, Jacob 18
creeds 10, 15, 23, 27, 49
cross 13, 64, 66, 115, 117,
120-123, 133-135, 137
Crusades 153

## D

defense
20, 22, 36, 38, 71, 80, 88, 89,
97, 99, 102, 106, 108, 109, 110,
111, 112, 122, 125, 133,
134, 148, 153
Disciplesof Christ
6, 9-15, 18, 26-
27, 38, 52,57, 65, 67, 96,
117, 118, 120, 123,
129, 131, 135-136, 150
disobedience
5, 87, 89, 90, 91, 94, 98, 100
dispensations
23, 24, 26, 27, 28, 41,
46, 47, 97, 109, 150
Dodge, David Low 21, 26, 27, 70-71
Dymond, Jonathan 22

## E

Eames, S Morris 39, 43
Edwards, Jonathan 21
Enlightenment 21, 39, 41, 73
Episcopalians 11
ethics 19, 27, 45, 53-55, 67,
77, 105, 115, 123, 137

## F


Fall, Phillip 18
Fanning, Tolbert 18
Franklin, Benjamin 18
Fugitive Slave Law
91, 93, 94, 95, 96, 98


## G


Garrison, William Lloyd
46, 71, 85, 100
Garrison, W.E. 45, 47
George H. Corey 35
Golden Rule 95, 97
Gorman, Michael 121
Grimké, Thomas S.
22, 23, 27, 62, 70, 71, 104, 111, 161


## H


Hall, William S. 75
Harrell, David Edwin, Jr.
9, 15, 27, 51, 57, 65, 68
Hartford Peace Society 61
Holmes, Abiel 70
horrors of war 39, 139, 154
Hugo, M.V. 43


## J


Jenyns, Soame
20, 54, 63, 75, 82, 118
just war 10, 22, 36, 128, 129


## K


kingdom
8, 21, 24, 26, 33, 34, 35, 37, 38, 41, 42, 45-48, 52, 54, 57,66, 70, 74, 77, 79, 82, 88, 110, 124, 125, 132, 133, 135-137, 143-147, 151


## L


Ladd, William
22, 61, 73, 85, 104, 130
Lard, Moses 18
League of Universal Brotherhood
61
Legalism 53
Locke, John
41, 60, 74, 85, 88
Luther 41, 88


## M


Massachusetts Peace Society
21, 36, 69, 152
McCorkle, Samuel M. 41
Methodists 11
Mexican-American War 12
*Millennial Harbinger*
11, 15, 18, 22, 27, 28, 29, 42, 43, 49, 51, 57, 67, 68, 81, 85, 86, 87, 88, 89, 93, 97, 100, 101, 106, 112, 113, 114, 115, 137, 139
millennium
42, 45, 46, 48-52, 56, 57, 59, 60, 61, 64-66, 77, 132, 135
Milton, John 60
moral socieities 78-79
Moses
18, 23, 24, 47, 110, 146 149
murder
99, 102, 104, 106, 107, 109, 111, 113, 145, 146, 148, 158, 161


## N


Napoleon
36, 38, 139, 148 150, 154, 156
New England Non-Resistant Society 71
New York Peace Society 21, 70

Newton, Isaac 41
Niebuhr, H. Richard
48, 57, 117, 137
non-resistants
46, 72, 83, 87, 88, 89, 93
nonviolence
10, 11, 12, 14, 20, 27, 31, 32, 35, 42, 45, 52, 65, 71, 80, 87, 105, 113, 124, 130, 134, 135

## O

Owen, Robert
20, 28, 50, 53, 57, 568 63, 67, 85

## P

patriotism 20, 34, 63-64, 156
Phillips, William 21, 69
police action 79, 102
Presbyterians 9-11, 17-21, 27, 75

## R

Richardson, Robert
18, 19, 28, 50, 57, 85

## S

science
12, 41, 48 59, 74, 75, 78, 87, 90, 94, 96, 100,140, 141, 144, 157, 159, 160
Seceder Presbyterians 18, 19, 27
Sermon on the Mount
26, 87, 105, 110
slavery
5, 25, 83, 87, 91, 92, 93, 94, 95, 96, 97, 98, 99, 101
Stone, Barton 10, 18

## T

Tertullian 112, 160
theocracy 31, 145, 148, 158

## U

United States of America
4, 5, 10, 11, 13, 14, 15, 17, 21, 23, 28, 29, 34, 40, 43, 45, 48, 56, 57, 59, 60, 61, 62, 63, 64, 66, 67, 74, 76, 83, 84, 90, 96, 97 99, 100, 113, 114, 126, 137, 143, 144, 147, 158, 160

unity of the Church
4, 8, 12, 17, 21, 25, 33, 35, 39, 45, 48, 49, 52, 59, 60, 63, 82, 84, 92, 94, 99, 124, 125, 126, 127, 128, 132, 143, 144, 147
Upham, Thomas 52, 71, 83

## W

Washington Moral Society 78
Wayland, Francis
45, 56, 89, 100
Westminister Confession 10
Westminster Abbey 156
Wheaton, N.S. 61
Worcester, Noah 21, 69
Wright, Henry Clark 46 , 72

## Z

Zwingli 41